JOHN T

THE KINGDOM EQUATION

A FRESH LOOK AT THE
PARABLES OF JESUS

CRC Publications
Grand Rapids, Michigan

Printed in the United States of America.
10 9 8 7 6 5 4 3

Library of Congress Cataloging-in-Publication Data
Timmer, John, 1927-
The kingdom equation: a fresh look at the parables of Jesus / John Timmer.
    p. cm.
Includes bibliographical references.
ISBN 0-930265-87-4
1. Jesus Christ—Parables. 2. Kingdom of God—Biblical teaching. I. Title.
BT375.2.T58 1990
226.8'06—dc20   90-33643

Contents

Preface

In recent years the Christian church has begun again to appreciate the deep importance of stories and storytelling. Even though the Bible is full of stories, for many decades—even centuries—we tended to view story as a lower form of truth, fit only for primitives and children. But recently, in pulpit and church school, story has emerged again as a unique and vital way of telling about God's saving work in Israel and the gospel of Jesus Christ.

Given that renewed appreciation, it is fitting that we take a fresh look at the stories Jesus told—the parables.

The author, Dr. John Timmer, brings to this book the latest in the study of language and its functions, in biblical interpretation, and in cultural sensitivity. He reviews and critiques the typical ways of looking at the parables and presents an interpretation of parable as metaphor.

Parables, says Timmer, are indirect teachings that help us grasp the new in terms of the old, the unknown by the known, the unfamiliar kingdom of God through familiar life scenes and experiences. A parable paints a picture of God's kingdom. It is a "kingdom equation."

In the twelve chapters of this book, Timmer applies this metaphor approach to a number of Jesus' parables, ranging from the story of the sower to the tale of the friend at midnight. In each of these stories of Jesus, our traditional notions are challenged and our values shockingly reversed.

John Timmer is a graduate of Calvin College and Seminary. He earned advanced degrees from Hartford Theological Seminary (S.T.M.) and the Free University of Amsterdam (Th.D.). He worked as missionary in Japan for fourteen years and is presently pastor of the Woodlawn Christian Reformed Church in Grand Rapids, Michigan.

To aid in using this book in a class situation, we have developed an accompanying leader's guide. This guide was written by Mr. Andy De Jong, pastor of the Covenant Life Church in Grand Haven, Michigan.

Harvey A. Smit
Editor in chief
Education Department

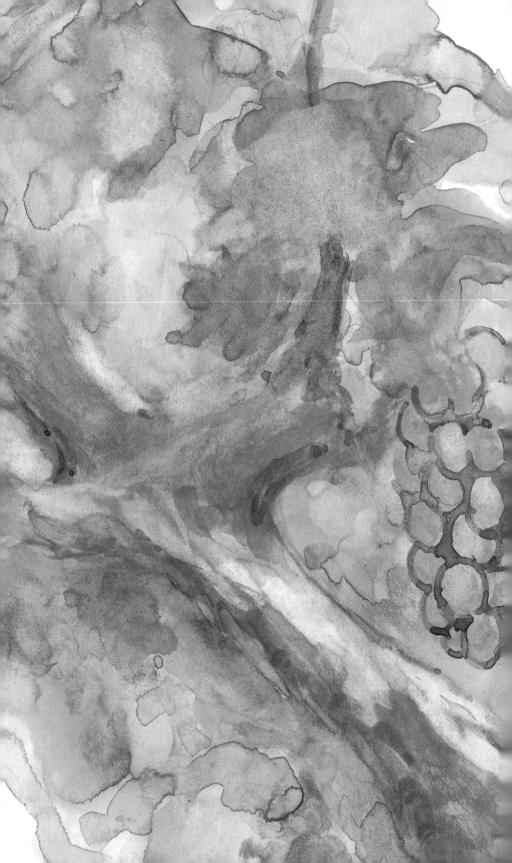

CHAPTER ONE

What Are Parables?

Jesus often told parables to the people who gathered to listen to him. "The kingdom of heaven is like a mustard seed," he would say to them. Or, "The kingdom of heaven is like a king who prepared a wedding banquet for his son."

Some of these parables were one-liners: "The kingdom of heaven is like yeast that a woman took and mixed into a large amount of flour until it worked all through the dough" (Matt. 13:33). Others, like the parable of the Good Samaritan, were short, compressed stories. But whatever their size or shape, each parable had a special message for those who listened. Jesus "did not say anything" to the people he spoke to "without using a parable" (Mark 4:34).

Why did Jesus use parables to teach his followers about God and his kingdom? Was it because it was popular in that first century Jewish culture to convey life's deepest mysteries through stories and parables? Or was there a deeper reason? What are the special dynamics of a parable? What *is* a parable?

People have defined the word *parable* in many different ways. Some say a parable is an

7

"illustrative story." Others define it as "an earthly story with a heavenly meaning," "an allegory," or "a story that makes a single point."

An Illustration?

The rabbis of Jesus' day viewed parables as illustrative stories that helped listeners understand an obscure point or a general truth—much as today's sermon illustrations do. They used parables to clarify difficult points in their teachings or to explain difficult passages of Scripture.

But Jesus did not teach in the same way as the rabbis of his day. He did not reduce the parable to an illustrative device that carries no message of its own. He viewed the parable not as an appetizer but as the main meal, not as an illustration of the gospel but as the gospel itself.

An Earthly Story with a Heavenly Meaning?

By far the most popular definition of the term *parable* is "an earthly story with a heavenly meaning." But this description, too, is misleading if we mean by it that Jesus used these earthly stories to focus our minds on heavenly things.

Parables do not draw comparisons between earth below and heaven above, but between our world and God's world. They seek not to make us disdain this present life for the sake of life after death, but rather to open our eyes to the presence of God's world inside our world of everyday experiences.

Parables, writes Edward Schillebeeckx,

> do not just point to another world beyond this one, but to a new possibility in this world, our world: to a real possibility of beginning to see and experience life and the

world in quite a different way from the usual one.

—*God Among Us,* 29

An Allegory?

From the beginning of the Christian era until about the twentieth century, Jesus' parables were widely treated as allegories: coded stories that veil their message in secrecy.

In an allegory everything stands for something else and is intelligible only to those who have cracked the code. To those who haven't, the allegory remains an obscure tale. All they can do is wait in patience or frustration for someone to decode it.

A classic example of reading the parable as allegory is St. Augustine's interpretation of the parable of the good Samaritan as found in Luke 10:30-35:

> The *man* is Adam, that is, humankind.
> *Jerusalem* is the heavenly city of peace, from whose blessedness Adam fell.
> *Jericho* stands for the moon. It signifies our mortality because, like the moon, it waxes and wanes.
> The *robbers* are the devil and his angels who strip Adam of his immortality.
> They *beat him* by persuading Adam to sin, leaving him half dead—that is, alive in so far as he can know God, but dead in so far as he is in the power of sin.
> The *priest* and the *Levite* represent the law and the prophets, which do not lead to salvation.
> The *Samaritan* personifies Jesus.
> The *bandaging of wounds* is the restraint of sin.
> The *oil* is the comfort of Christian

hope.

The *wine* is the admonition to persevere.

The *donkey* is the flesh in which Jesus comes to us.

Being put on the donkey is belief in the incarnation of Christ.

The *inn* is the church.

The *innkeeper* is the apostle Paul.

The *next day* is the day of Jesus' resurrection and the time after his resurrection.

The *two silver coins* are either the two commandments of love or the promise of this life and that which is to come.

This way of interpreting the parable of the good Samaritan, writes C. H. Dodd, prevailed down to the time of Archbishop Trench who, in his widely read *Notes on the Parables of Our Lord* (1841), follows its main outlines.

What is wrong with treating parables as allegories? Basically, two things.

First, such treatment is arbitrary. Interpreters have a standing invitation to read their own theology into the parable. Second, once the "coded" text of the parable has been translated into a text that can be understood by itself, the parable becomes dispensable.

A parable can never be dispensed with, for it expresses what cannot be expressed in any better way. Each translation of a parable always says less than the parable itself.

A Story That Makes a Single Point?

Still another way of viewing parables is Adolf Julicher's "one-point theory," popular when I went to seminary in the 1950s. Each parable, Julicher claimed, has but one point of comparison.

All the other elements of the parable only serve to enhance that one point and have no independent meaning of their own, the way they do in an allegory.

The meaning of a parable, Julicher said in effect, is like a drop of oil in water. Once the oil drop has been removed, the water can be dispensed with. Once the one-point meaning of the parable has been extracted, the parable serves no further purpose.

This theory, too, is inaccurate. The meaning of a parable cannot be reduced to a single point that, like a drop of oil, floats on the surface of the story. Rather, meaning is dispersed throughout the parable.

The Parable as Story Metaphor

Recent parable studies view parables primarily as *story metaphors*.

One of the most famous metaphors of our time is the one President John F. Kennedy used on his visit to West Berlin in 1963. In a speech delivered within sight of the Berlin Wall, Kennedy told the beleaguered citizens of West Berlin: "Ich bin ein Berliner" (I am a Berliner), and his metaphor electrified the people of that city.

A metaphor sees one thing as something else. It pretends, for example, that President Kennedy is a Berlin citizen, that the Lord is a shepherd, and that Jesus is a vine.

A metaphor uses language playfully. It equates the unknown with the known, the unfamiliar with the familiar. Thus, in Luke 13:32, Jesus compares Herod (the unknown and the unfamiliar) with a fox (the known and the familiar).

Jesus' language is shot through with metaphors. He called himself a vine, a door, bread, a shepherd, and the resurrection. He called Simon a rock, and

James and John sons of thunder. He piled metaphor upon metaphor in announcing the dawning of the kingdom of God.

Is and Is Not

A metaphor is an equation that is true and not true at the same time: "Herod is a fox," for example, or "The Lord is my shepherd," or "Jesus is the resurrection."

When President Kennedy said, "I am a Berliner," he meant that if the Russians would attack West Berlin, he would defend that city as though he were a native Berliner. He was, of course, not a real Berliner—he was an American. Similarly, Herod is and is not a fox. He is a fox in that he is as sly as that animal. He is not a fox in that he is a human being.

The "is" and "is not" dimensions of a metaphor function as two opposite poles that are in constant tension with each other—a tension that draws and repels, that joins and keeps separate. This tension can never be resolved, for by nature a good metaphor is inexhaustible. As Richard Berryman puts it, "Explanations satisfy momentarily, but metaphors haunt for a lifetime." A good metaphor can never be fully explained. Something always remains after the explaining is done.

Shock! Shock!

A good metaphor shocks, as did Kennedy's words to the people of Berlin. It brings together ideas that have never been brought together before. It upsets conventional language.

When Isaiah compared God to a whistler and to a barber (Isa. 7:18,20) and when Hosea declared that God is "like a moth to Ephraim, like rot to the people of Judah" (Hos. 5:12), these prophets used imagery that would never have occurred to the average God-fearing Israelite. God

had never been called any of these things before. This was language that shocked.

However, when metaphors are used too often, their shock value wears off. What once was a fresh and startling image becomes faded and worn.

A metaphor usually passes through three successive stages. In the first stage the unconventional language shocks and creates new insight. In the second stage the shocking metaphor becomes flat and commonplace. In the third stage the metaphor loses its sharp cutting edge and turns into a dead image.

Our everyday language is full of dead metaphors. We speak of a needle's eye, a chair's back, a bottle's neck, the arm of the law, the foot of a mountain, and the mouth of a river, never stopping to think that once upon a time each of these metaphors made people prick up their ears in surprise.

God and Metaphors

Almost all of the language the Bible uses to describe God is metaphorical. Ordinarily we are not aware of this, just as ordinarily we are not aware of the lenses of the glasses on our noses.

A metaphor is like a lens. When we look at something through a lens, we concentrate on what we are looking at and ignore the lens itself. But the next time you read a passage from Scripture, try to look *at* the lens rather than *through* it. Notice how God is called "king" or "judge" or "husband" or "wife" or "mother chicken" or "mother" or "shepherd" or "farmer" or "shelter" or "deceptive brook" or "lion tearing its prey to pieces."

There seems to be no end to the number of metaphors the Bible uses to describe God. The Scriptures seem to challenge us to examine the different facets of God through each one of these metaphors and notice what we have never noticed before.

Out of this abundance of metaphors, religious tradition always tends to prefer some over others. When major changes take place in that tradition, the choice of metaphors for God changes as well. We in the Reformed tradition, for example, are beginning to recognize that for several generations we have one-sidedly used some metaphors for God and neglected others. As a result, our emerging image of God is somewhat different from the one many of us grew up with. Three things contribute toward this shift in God metaphors:

1. *Science and technology*. Pick up an old hymnbook. You will notice that many of the metaphors for God are rural, reflecting the kind of society we used to be. Today, under the influence of science and technology, our hymns contain such metaphors as "God of concrete, God of steel, God of piston and of wheel, God of pylon, God of steam, God of girder and of beam."

2. *Black and liberation theology*. Both black and liberation theology have focused needed attention on metaphors that picture God as the liberator of the poor and the oppressed.

3. *Women's movement*. This movement has exposed the unjustified predominance of male metaphors for God in hymn books, in Bible translations, in the creeds, and in Christian and theological literature.

Why So Many Metaphors?

Why does our language, or any language for that matter, contain so many living and dead metaphors? Partly because we need the old to name and describe the new.

Suppose you had never before in your life seen a chair. How would you go about describing one? You could not do much better than what people did when they named the four things on which a chair stands "legs," the part you lean against the "back," and the parts you rest your arms on "arms." You could do no better, that is, than describing the unfamiliar chair in terms of your familiar body.

This is precisely what metaphors do. They seek to capture the new and unknown by means of the old and familiar.

To grow in any knowledge, whether of science or of the Christian faith, we are dependent on metaphors. A metaphor pushes us to organize our thoughts about the less familiar, helping us see it in terms of the more familiar. Haven't you ever wondered why the Bible describes the unfamiliar future God has promised in terms of such familiar expressions as "the new exodus," "the new covenant," "the new Jerusalem," and "the new creation"?

Parable as Metaphor

A metaphor reveals something new. It offers a fresh insight that cannot be expressed as well in any other way. It equates two things that have never been equated before.

Jesus uses this type of unusual equation in his parables. He equates the unfamiliar kingdom of God, for example, with familiar scenes of everyday life. The kingdom of God, he tells his listeners,

"is like treasure hidden in a field. When a man found it, he hid it again, and then in his joy went and sold all he had and bought that field." —*Matthew 13:44-45*

Jesus does not say, as some commentaries claim, that the kingdom is like a treasure. Not just the treasure, but the whole story lights up what the kingdom is about. That's why this book is called "The Kingdom Equation." Each parable, each equation, gives us a new insight into God's kingdom.

Even those parables—such as the prodigal son—that do not mention the kingdom of God teach about God's kingdom by implication. The silent assumption behind each of Jesus' parables is that life in the kingdom is the way it is portrayed in the plot of the parable.

Jesus' central message is: "The kingdom of God is near" (Mark 1:15). This kingdom breaks into our present life in shocking ways. Parables as descriptions of this kingdom action, therefore,

> shock the mind into opening to the unenvisioned possible; they madly exaggerate in order to jolt the consciousness of the religiously secure; they are an assault upon the obvious. The entire momentum of conventional piety is brought into question: the man sells everything for the one thing; the shepherd leaves the ninety-nine undefended in order to find the lost one; in defiance of common sense, the woman takes the house apart to find the lost coin; the lord commends the unjust steward for his uncanny perception of the truth.
> —Joseph Sittler, *Gravity and Grace, 110*

Why in Parables?

We are now in a position to understand why Jesus chose the parable as his primary teaching device.

A parable is a metaphor, a story metaphor. And a metaphor is an equation. It equates something strange and unfamiliar with something known and familiar.

A parable equates the unfamiliar kingdom of God with a familiar scene or experience. At first the equation looks rather tame and harmless. "Oh," we say, "is that what the kingdom of God is?" But then we begin to reflect on the equation and before we know it, sparks begin to fly. We are caught in the field of tension between the "is" and "is not" of the metaphorical equation. "How can the kingdom of God be like *that?*" we ask. "How can it be like the behavior of that unjust steward?"

Clarence Jordan calls parables a sort of Trojan horse—a big wooden horse that the Greeks filled with soldiers and sent to the enemy city of Troy. When the people of Troy pulled this horse into the city, they saw or heard nothing unusual, for the threat was hidden inside. Late that night, however, when everybody was asleep, the hidden trapdoor on that horse opened, and the Greek soldiers jumped out. They ran to the city gates and opened them, and their fellow soldiers rushed in and captured the city.

Jesus' parables are like that Trojan horse. "There was a man who had two sons." So Jesus begins one of his parables, and then he proceeds to tell a story in the past tense about anonymous people in a faraway place. As we listen to this story, we relax and enjoy the telling of it. We assure ourselves, "There's nothing in this story that addresses *me*." But then it happens. After listening to the whole story, after having pulled the Trojan horse into our city, down comes the hidden trapdoor, and before we know it our lives are exposed and made vulnerable.

Why did Jesus teach in parables? To get through to people who are up to their ears in Scripture, who have heard it all before many times, who have memorized their catechism, who know their doctrine, who have sat before pulpits all their life.

How do you approach such people? How can you get through to them? How command a hearing for the gospel?

By telling parables—stories that start off on familiar ground and then catch them completely off guard.

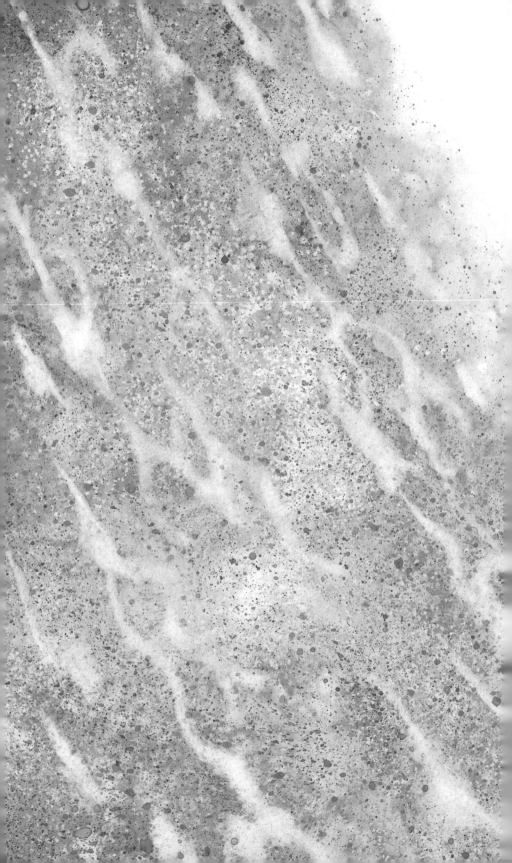

CHAPTER TWO

What Is the Kingdom of God?

When we begin reading the words of Jesus, it is easy to lose sight of the forest because of the trees.

We read a couple of sayings here, a parable there, a dispute with religious leaders somewhere else, and then begin to wonder what binds all of these together. What is their single focus? What central message is Jesus trying to get across?

As we search for an answer, we come upon a surprise. We find that Jesus' words are not first of all focused on himself, but rather on the kingdom of God. We discover that through his teachings and healings and miracles Jesus points toward the imminent arrival of God's kingdom.

That discovery raises a question: What *is* this kingdom of which Jesus speaks? And as we struggle with that question, we come upon the next surprise. We find that Jesus never defines the term *kingdom,* that he never offers the kind of description that prompts us to say: "Oh, is that what the kingdom of God is? Now I know!"

Only in Stories

Rather than offer a definition of *kingdom,* Jesus tells stories about it. For example, in Matthew 13:45-46 Jesus equates the kingdom with

"a merchant looking for fine pearls. When he found one of great value, he went away and sold everything he had and bought it."

Jesus tells many such stories— stories that paint pictures of the kingdom of God without offering precise descriptions of it. He tells so many stories that we begin to wonder why he doesn't come right out and tell us in clear

15

and unambiguous language what the kingdom is. Why does he talk about it only indirectly, in stories?

One answer is that we can never absorb strange and difficult truths directly. We can only learn of them indirectly.

Suppose someone asks you, "What is time?" You could not possibly answer that question directly. St. Augustine writes in his *Confessions*,

> I know what it [time] is if no one asks me what it is. But if I want to explain it to someone who has asked me, I find that I do not know.

Such a concept can only be explained indirectly: We can only say what time means to us and how it functions in our lives.

What is true of time is also true of the kingdom of God. To be seen at all, the idea of kingdom must be approached indirectly. To be understood at all, it is best described in story form.

In the previous chapter we noted that the easiest way to teach something new and unfamiliar is to explain it by metaphor. We can never absorb the deepest truths directly. We can only learn of them indirectly, with the help of metaphors that describe the unfamiliar in terms of the familiar.

We cannot describe God directly; only indirectly by means of metaphors. The Bible does this repeatedly when it calls God "king" or "mother" or "rock" or "sun." We cannot see God directly either. Looking at God directly would be like looking at the sun directly. It would blind us. In the same way, our vision of the kingdom cannot be direct. It can only be indirect, via parables.

Some Popular Views of the Kingdom

To gain a better understanding of the kingdom of God it is helpful to contrast Jesus' view of the kingdom with some popular distortions of it.

Social and Political Order

This well-known hymn reflects the common view of the kingdom as a new social and political order:

> Rise up, O men of God!
> His kingdom tarries long;
> Bring in the day of brotherhood,
> And end the night of wrong.

If this happens to be your view of the kingdom, you have no choice in the matter—you must do your utmost to bring in God's kingdom.

Significantly, Jesus never tells his followers to bring in the kingdom. What he tells them to do is pray for its coming: "Your kingdom come."

We do not *bring in* the kingdom of God. We receive it. We are accepted into it like the sheep at Christ's right hand or else are excluded from it like the goats at his left hand (Matt. 25:33, 34 and 41).

Future Millennium

A second popular view of the kingdom involves seeing it as a future millennium.

If this happens to be your view—if you conceive of the kingdom as something still hidden in the unknown future—then you are forced into regarding the present as being of little importance, a time to get through as quickly as possible so that we can reach the millennium.

In Our Hearts

A third popular view internalizes the kingdom. It says that the kingdom is the rule of God in the hearts of believers.

If this happens to be your view, much of your time and energy will go into protecting your inner spiritual life from outside influences. Your attitude toward life will be one of defense, withdrawal, and ghetto building.

Starting Point for Understanding

The beginning of wisdom in understanding the kingdom lies in going back to the Old Testament and listening to such representative voices as these:

Dominion belongs to the Lord and he rules over the nations. —*Psalm 22:28*

The Lord reigns, let the earth be glad; let the distant shores rejoice. —*Psalm 97:1*

"The Most High is sovereign over the kingdoms of men and gives them to anyone he wishes." —*Daniel 4:25*

The most beautiful and majestic statement of God's kingly rule, however, is found in Isaiah 40. Here the prophet asks,

Who has measured the waters in the hollow of his hand, or with the breadth of his hand marked off the heavens? Who has held the dust of the earth in a basket, or weighed the mountains on the scales and the hills in a balance? Who has understood the mind of the Lord, or instructed him as his counselor? Whom did the Lord consult to enlighten him, and who taught him the right way? Who was it that taught him knowledge or showed him the path of understanding? —*vv. 12-14*

Who? Who? Who? And the prophet's reply is

Do you not know? Have you not heard? Has it not been told you from the beginning? Have you not understood since the earth was founded? He sits enthroned above the circle of the earth, and its people are like grasshoppers. He stretches out the heavens like a canopy, and spreads them out like a tent to live in. He brings princes to naught and reduces the rulers of this world to nothing. —*vv. 21-23*

Isaiah 40 is one of the most powerful testimonies of God's universal rule. By affirming this rule it attacks the heart of paganism, both ancient and modern. It attacks the belief that there is something higher and mightier than God, something that is over God and to which God is subject. Call that higher something "fate." Call it "bad luck." Call it "good luck." It matters little. Each of these descriptions is a way of saying that there is something beyond and above God, something that controls God instead of God controlling it.

The heart of paganism—both past and present—is the denial that God rules over *all*. Over against this denial the Old Testament confesses that all things happen under the universal umbrella of God's kingly rule.

To the Old Testament, the best of the good news is that God rules over all. Therefore, when Jesus starts his ministry by proclaiming that "the kingdom of God is near," he is simply affirming the core proclamation of the Old Testament. Jesus is saying that with his coming, God is manifesting his kingly rule in a new way.

The Kingdom as Present and Future

In Jesus' proclamation of the kingdom, there is always a tension between the present reality of the kingdom and the future fullness of the kingdom. But Jesus' main emphasis is on the kingdom in the present:

"The kingdom of God is near."
                              —Mark 1:15

"If I drive out demons by the Spirit of God, then the kingdom of God has come upon you."   *—Matthew 12:28*

"The kingdom of God does not come with your careful observation, nor will people say, 'Here it is,' or 'There it is,' because the kingdom of God is within [among] you."   *—Luke 17:20-21*

The door to the future of God's full reign has been opened. In Christ, the future is already present. In him, the powers of the age to come have entered our lives, and we can already experience his kingdom in such things as his forgiveness of our sins.

We also experience the presence of God's kingdom each time we forgive someone else. God does not want us to live under the power furnished by this age. Doing so results in hating and resenting others, especially our enemies. Christ wants us to love and forgive them. He expects us to live by the power of the kingdom of God already available now. Each time we forgive someone—up to seventy times seven times—we demonstrate that the kingdom of God has come near, that the powers of the future age are already now shaping our behavior.

We also experience the presence of God's kingly rule through the breakdown of racial, social, and sexual barriers. In Christ there is neither Jew nor Greek, slave nor free, male nor female. Ancient society was divided by three forces—race, class, and sex. "No longer!" the New Testament proclaims. With the coming of Christ the power of God's kingly rule began the slow and hidden but irreversible process of demolishing these barriers. When the kingdom of God has come fully, these barriers to unity will be completely gone as well.

God's Present Rule Is Hidden

Suppose someone were to hand you a camera and ask you to take pictures of scenes that clearly show God's rule over all things. You soon would feel frustrated, for God's rule is a hidden one. God's rule, writes Günther Bornkamm,

> is hidden from us, and must be believed and understood in its hiddenness. Not in the way the apocalypticists thought, beyond the heavens, in the bosom of a mysterious future, but here, hidden in the everyday world of the present time, where no one is aware of what is already taking place. Of this Jesus speaks in his parables of the kingdom of God.
> —*Jesus of Nazareth*, 69

Jesus' parables speak of the hidden dawn of the kingdom of God in a world which, to human eyes, shows no trace of that kingdom. Let us briefly look at three of these parables.

The Parable of the Seed Growing Secretly

"This is what the kingdom of God is like. A man scatters seed on the ground. Night and day, whether he sleeps or gets up, the seed sprouts and grows, though he does not know how. All by itself the soil produces grain—first the stalk, then the head, then the full kernel in the head. As soon as the grain is ripe, he puts the sickle to it, because the harvest has come."
—Mark 4:26-29

What gives focus to this parable? Is it what happens to the seed? Is it the progressive and irresistible growth of the seed whose inner power overcomes all obstacles and does not need the farmer once it has been sown?

Probably not. It seems the action of the seed is only a subplot bracketed between the actions of the farmer—between his scattering of the seed and his harvesting of the grain.

Actually the parable focuses on the behavior of the farmer, on his action and his non-action, on his usual behavior of sowing and harvesting and his unusual behavior of not interfering with the growing seed.

Jesus is saying that God is like that farmer. Even though he is working all the time, at present he is doing so in a hidden way. He seems to be passive and unconcerned, like the farmer who gets up and goes to bed and does not seem to care.

But in the fullness of time, God will exhibit his rule for all to see.

The Parable of the Mustard Seed

"What shall we say the kingdom of God is like, or what parable shall we use to describe it? It is like a mustard seed, which is the smallest seed you plant in the

ground. Yet when planted, it grows and becomes the largest of all garden plants, with such big branches that the birds of the air can perch in its shade."
—Mark 4:30-32

This parable, too, speaks of the kingdom as present in hidden form and as developing toward fullness. it directs us to the world of daily experiences where magnificent things are hidden in insignificant things and where the greatest is hidden in the smallest.

God's kingdom is hidden in the small and insignificant. It is at work in hidden fashion in the most ordinary events.

The Parable of the Yeast

"The kingdom of heaven is like yeast that a woman took and mixed into a large amount of flour until it worked all through the dough." *—Matthew 13:33*

The kingly rule of God, Jesus says, is like the entire leavening process. Hidden from the human eye, the yeast permeates the whole lump of dough and does its work.

Jesus had often watched his mother bake bread. He had often seen her take yeast and mix it in with the dough—with amazing results. For the yeast, though hidden inside the mass of dough, greatly changes the shape and texture of the dough. At first nothing appears to happen. But then, slowly on, the dough begins to swell and bubble.

The kingdom of God is like that. It is a hidden force in the dead lump of humanity. Looking at the world we say easily: "What a corrupt world we're living in! What a crowd of self-seeking people we are!" True! But also true is that, mixed in with this corrupt world and selfish crowd is yeast capable of changing and transforming everything.

It may take centuries, but things will eventually change. The yeast will do its work.

Look, for example, at the great changes that have come about in the way men relate to women. In Jesus' day, being a woman was not much fun. Like slaves, women were pieces of property, owned either by their father or their husband. They were without legal rights.

Here comes Jesus, and what does he do? He brings women before God on an equal footing with men. He accords men and women equal status before God. Against all custom, and in violation of religious law, he makes women his friends, teaches them the Torah, spends time with them in public and in private, and entrusts to them his single most important task: the witness to his resurrection.

By doing all these things, Jesus mixed kingdom yeast in with a male-dominated society. Slowly and imperceptibly, for many centuries, this yeast permeated that society, until in our day we are able to see the swelling and the bubbling. During the past few decades denominations have struggled seriously with the issue of the role of women in the church and many of them concluded that, yes, women should serve in as many areas as possible, on committees and boards and church councils.

Why? Because we have slowly come to see that what we are dealing with is not secular yeast but kingdom yeast.

"The kingdom of God is like yeast that a woman took and mixed into a large amount of flour . . . ."

CHAPTER THREE

The Jesus Parable

"A farmer went out to sow his seed. As he was scattering the seed, some fell along the path, and the birds came and ate it up. Some fell on rocky places, where it did not have much soil. It sprang up quickly, because the soil was shallow. But when the sun came up, the plants were scorched, and they withered because they had no root. Other seed fell among thorns, which grew up and choked the plants, so that they did not bear grain. Still other seed fell on good soil. It came up, grew and produced a crop, multiplying thirty, sixty, or even a hundred times."

—Mark 4:3-8

The first parable to which we will devote an entire chapter is the well-known parable of the sower. It deserves priority treatment because of what Jesus says to his disciples in Mark 4:13: "Don't you understand this parable? How then will you understand any parable?" The sower parable provides the key to Jesus' other parables.

Focusing the Sower Parable

You will recall from the first chapter that a parable is an equation—a kingdom equation. A parable equates two worlds—God's world and our world. It equates the unfamiliar kingdom of God with a familiar human scene. In the case of the sower parable, the parable equates the kingly rule of God with the story of a sower sowing seed on different kinds of soil. It tells us how God's kingly rule enters our world and works within that world. The focal point of the parable is what the *sower* does, not how the various kinds of soil receive seed.

If we focus the parable on the various kinds of soil—on the different ways in which people react to the word of God—then the basic questions the parable asks would be these: What kind of soil are you? Hard-beaten, rocky, thorny, or good soil? Is your mind closed toward the gospel? Is your faith shallow? Does your life crowd out the gospel, or are you open to it?

If we focus the parable on what people do and on how they react to the word of God, then the parable teaches that even though God's word is always good, the effect it has depends on the condition of the heart into which it falls. What people do rather than what God does stands at the center of attention.

But if we focus the parable on what the sower does, then the parable is about the vulnerable and offensive way in which the kingdom of God enters our world.

Why in Parables?

After Jesus told the parable of the sower, the disciples asked him privately about the parables (Mark 4:10). They asked him why he spoke to people in parables (Matt.13:10).

The disciples' question, writes Herman Ridderbos in his book *The Coming of the Kingdom,* can hardly mean that the parable as a teaching device was unknown or unusual. It can hardly mean that the disciples are wondering why Jesus doesn't channel his teachings through a more popular teaching medium. After all, the rabbis of Jesus' day also taught in parables, though they used them for different purposes.

What bothers the disciples is that Jesus does not express his thoughts directly, without the use of parables. They are asking Jesus, "Why take such a roundabout route? Why not spell it out in clear and unambiguous language?" Jesus answers the disciples by explaining,

"The secret of the kingdom of God has been given to you. But to those on the outside everything is said in parables so that 'they may be ever seeing but never perceiving, and ever hearing but never understanding . . .'"   —Mark 4:11-12

The parables Jesus tells only make sense to those who know "the secret of the kingdom"—to those who know that the kingdom of God has come in Jesus and with Jesus. To know the secret of the kingdom is to know that salvation is present in Jesus. Jesus' parables cannot be understood without this knowledge because Jesus himself cannot be understood without it.

The parables do not make sense to those who "see but do not perceive." To understand the difference between seeing and perceiving, recall the story in John 20 of Peter and John running to the tomb on Easter morning.

John reaches the tomb first. He bends over to look in and sees the strips of linen lying there.

The Greek word used to describe John's seeing is *blepo,* a verb that describes what happens when you turn your head in a certain direction and keep your eyes open.

John turns his head in the direction of the inside tomb and sees (*blepo)* the strips of linen.

Then John enters the tomb, and he sees and believes that Jesus has risen.

The Greek verb used to describe this seeing is *horao. Horao* is not just "seeing" but "discerning." When you "see" in the *horao* sense, something breaks in on you, light dawns on you.

These two Greek verbs for seeing—*blepo* and *horao*—also occur in Mark 4:12, where Jesus tells his disciples that he communicates in parables to those who do not know "the secret of the kingdom," so that "they may be ever seeing [*blepo*] but never perceiving [*horao*]."

To those who know "the secret of the kingdom," Jesus' parables are revelations about himself: Jesus is the sower, and in Jesus the kingdom of God enters our world. To those who do *not* know that secret, these same parables are nothing but stories that are bound to leave them puzzled and confused.

The Kingdom as Sown Seed

The sower sows the seed, which is the word that Jesus proclaims on earth (Mark 4:14). It is the word in which he announces that the kingdom of God has come.

But how has the kingdom come? And how is it still coming today?

The sower parable announces that the kingdom comes as sown seed comes to the soil, looking very weak and vulnerable. Like sown seed, the word announcing the arrival of the kingdom can easily be trodden underfoot, snatched away, or choked.

Again, the kingdom comes like a sower. And a sower is the most dependent person imaginable. A sower surrenders the seed to a variety of variables—the soil, the weather, the sun, birds, and weeds. All a sower can do after sowing the seed is wait and see what will become of it. The sun, the rain, the wind, the birds, the weeds—all begin to act on the seed that now lies vulnerably exposed.

The way in which the kingdom comes makes both Jesus and the word he preaches offensive to people who have their own ideas about how God's kingdom ought to come. It makes Jesus and his kingdom word offensive to people who believe that the kingdom comes at the end of history as we now know it and that it will come suddenly and with judgment. What, such people ask, will become of the kingdom when it comes like a sower sowing seed, when it is surrendered to American soil, to Russian soil, or to Iranian soil? Who will protect the seed to keep it from being trodden underfoot or from being choked?

Parable of Hope

It is easy to feel pessimistic about the future outcome of God's kingdom when we think of it coming like a sower sowing seed. "Look at all that wasted seed," we might say. "Look at all the obstacles the kingdom must overcome."

The disciples must have said or thought the same thing—especially when they observed the way others reacted to Jesus. The Pharisees in alliance with the Herodians were seeking to destroy Jesus (Mark 3:6). Jesus' own family doubted his sanity and thought he was beside himself (Mark 3:21). And the scribes accused him of colluding with the prince of demons. With so much opposition and misunderstanding to block its path, what chance did the kingdom really have to succeed?

Sometimes we feel like the disciples did. With the retreat of Christianity in the Western world the kingdom seems to be going, not coming. The widespread apostasy, the spiritual apathy, and the wholesale breakdown of public morality makes us say the opposite of what the sower parable is saying.

The kingdom of God comes like seed sown upon the ground. It comes like a sower sowing seed. Both Jesus the sower and the kingdom word he sows will always appear weak and vulnerable to the uninitiated, to those who do not know "the secret of the kingdom of God."

The sower parable, however, is not pessimistic in the least about the final harvest. Considering that seed multiplying ten times is an average crop, you can well imagine how seed multiplying thirty times or sixty times or even a hundred times will make any farmer rejoice.

The sower parable is extremely optimistic about the future God has promised. It points us to the incredible germinal force of the seed.

Reactions to the Seed

The kingdom of God comes like a sower sowing seed. It runs into the same kind of resistance and opposition that sown seed runs into.

What kind of resistance and opposition is that? How, in fact, did people react to Jesus' ministry?

In his sower parable, Jesus divides people into four categories: hard-soil people, rocky-soil people, thorny- soil people, and good-soil people. These four categories, which reflect the way people

respond to the word, are not necessarily permanent states. By repenting, a rocky-soil person can become a good-soil person. So can a hard-soil and a thorny-soil person. In other words, we must allow room for change.

At some time in our life we might think, as the members of Jesus' family did, that Jesus is "out of his mind" (Mark 3:21). At a later time we may change, as Jesus' brother James did after the outpouring of the Holy Spirit on Pentecost.

We must keep this fluidity in mind as we consider the four categories.

Hard-Soil People

Some people reject Jesus and what he teaches outright. They are like the hard-beaten path that refuses to receive the seed. They are like the Pharisees who in Mark 3:6 seek ways to destroy Jesus. They are like the scribes in Mark 3:22 who ascribe Jesus' exorcisms to Satan.

Rocky-Soil People

Other people begin by following Jesus but fall away when tribulation or persecution comes. These are the ones who

"hear the word and at once receive it with joy. But since they have no root, they last only a short time. When trouble or persecution comes because of the word, they quickly fall away." —Mark 4:16-17

Who are some of these rocky-soil people? We may think of the people in Mark 11:18, who are amazed at Jesus' teaching one day and shout "Crucify him!" the next day.

We may also think of the people Jesus mentions in Mark 13:12, people who, under pressure of persecution, betray those who are closest to them.

"Brother will betray brother to death, and a father his child. Children will rebel against their parents and have them put to death."

Do Jesus' disciples fall into this rocky-soil category? At first sight, it appears that way. For when Jesus was arrested in the Garden of Gethsemane, they all "deserted him and fled" (Mark 14:50).

When seen in the broader context of Mark's gospel, however, this way of categorizing the disciples proves to be wrong. A number of factors indicate that the disciples (with the exception of Judas) do not, in the end, belong to the group of bad-soil people but to the good-soil people.

For example, in Mark 10:28-31 Jesus contrasts the disciples favorably to the rich man. While the rich man has been led astray by the deceitfulness of wealth, the disciples have given up home and family for the sake of the gospel and will therefore receive the hundredfold reward of the kingdom. And in Mark 13:9-13 Jesus predicts that the disciples will suffer much hatred and persecution for his sake, but that in the midst of this persecution, they will preach the gospel with the power of the Holy Spirit.

The disciples therefore are good-soil people, for they hear the word Jesus preaches, accept it, and produce an abundant crop.

Thorny-Soil People

These are the people who crowd their lives with so many things—many of them very worthwhile—that Jesus gets crowded out. They are so busy making money and paying off their debts, so busy planning their futures and advancing their careers, that they have no time to reflect on *how* they live. They hear the word,

"but the worries of this life, the deceitfulness of wealth and the desires for other things come in and choke the word, making it unfruitful."   —*Mark 4:18-19*

Thorny-soil people are those who, like the rich man in Mark 10:17-22, are seduced by riches into making the wrong choice concerning the kingdom of God.

Good-Soil People

Finally, there are those who receive the word of God the way Mary did. They keep it in their hearts and ponder over it. In such lives the seeds germinate, grow, ripen, and bring forth much fruit.

The sower parable reflects the ministry of Jesus like a mirror. The things he mentions in this parable—Satan coming and taking away the word that was sown, persecution causing apostasy, love of money choking the word—are actually taking place in his ministry. Each reaction to the seed in the sower parable has its parallel in the ministry of Jesus. In other words, the parable of the sower is autobiographical. It can rightly be called the Jesus parable.

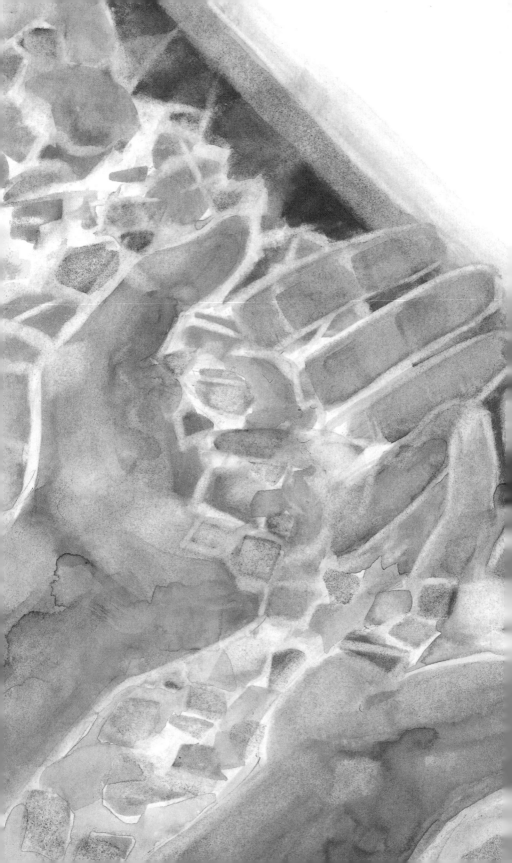

CHAPTER FOUR

The Hidden Treasure

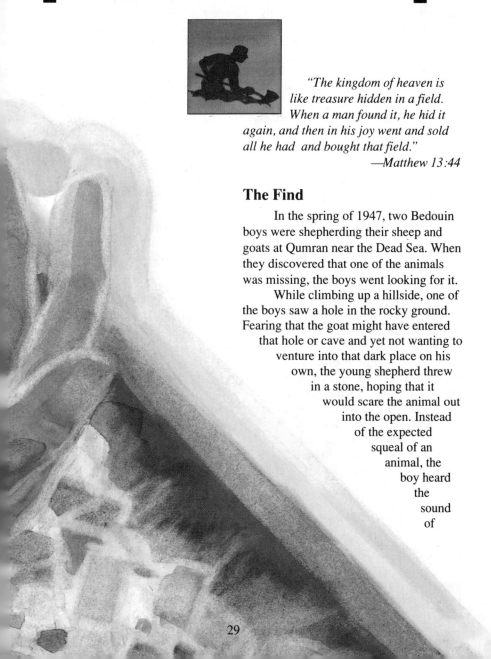

"The kingdom of heaven is like treasure hidden in a field. When a man found it, he hid it again, and then in his joy went and sold all he had and bought that field."
—*Matthew 13:44*

The Find

In the spring of 1947, two Bedouin boys were shepherding their sheep and goats at Qumran near the Dead Sea. When they discovered that one of the animals was missing, the boys went looking for it.

While climbing up a hillside, one of the boys saw a hole in the rocky ground. Fearing that the goat might have entered that hole or cave and yet not wanting to venture into that dark place on his own, the young shepherd threw in a stone, hoping that it would scare the animal out into the open. Instead of the expected squeal of an animal, the boy heard the sound of

29

breaking pottery. Frightened, he ran off to find his buddy.

Together the boys returned to the hole and crept into the cave. As their eyes adjusted to the darkness inside, they saw some earthenware jars. Stuffed inside were rolls and rolls of ancient scrolls.

The boys' discovery touched off a thorough search of the area. Eventually eleven caves were discovered, yielding up over six hundred scrolls and thousands of fragments from scrolls. About one-third of these turned out to be biblical writings.

In going about their daily duty, the two boys had unexpectedly come upon one of the biggest archeological treasures of modern times. They had found the first of the now famous Dead Sea Scrolls.

Some nineteen centuries earlier, roughly fifty miles to the north as the crow flies, near the Sea of Galilee, Jesus had told a somewhat similar story about someone going about his daily duty and suddenly coming upon a treasure.

A man was working a field when he came upon a treasure that, years ago, someone had hidden there to preserve it from plundering soldiers or from thieves.

Palestine was a land of wars. Often and unexpectedly it became a battlefield, and houses were looted. In a day in which there were no banks, burying money and valuables was the safest protection against plunder and theft. The rabbis even had a saying for it: "There is only one safe repository of money—the earth."

If the owner died before he could disclose the hiding place to his heirs, the treasure lay hidden and forgotten in the earth until a lucky finder discovered it.

The Kingdom Is Like . . .

The kingdom of heaven is not merely like treasure hidden in a field.

Rather, it must be understood in terms of the *entire* parable. It is "like treasure hidden in a field. When a man found it, he hid it again, and then in his joy went and sold all he had and bought that field." What does this mean? What does the entire parable reveal about the kingdom? More specifically, what does it say about the when and where of the kingdom?

What this parable makes clear is that the kingdom is not something up in the blue yonder. It is not a "glory land, way beyond the blue."

Nor is the kingdom of heaven something that is still hidden in the bosom of the future, something yet to come. It is not like the millennium, as understood by premillennialists—a thousand-year rule of peace and justice to be set up by Christ after his second coming.

The kingdom of God, rather, is something that has already broken into our present world. It is hidden in the most ordinary places and in the most ordinary events. It is as close to us as the treasure was close to the plowing man who, as Helmut Thielicke writes,

> was probably dismayed at first when his plow struck an obstacle. His first outburst may have been, "Oh, these confounded stones!"

How This Works in Real Life

A Certain Ruler

What if? What if Jesus had first told this parable to the ruler who asked him, "Good teacher, what must I do to inherit eternal life?" (Luke 18:18). What reaction would Jesus have evoked?

The treasure the ruler was searching for was "eternal life." Somehow he thought this treasure was far away. In actuality, he was looking right at it. It was Jesus.

Jesus asked him, "Are you willing to sell all that you have for the sake of this treasure? Are you willing to dispose of all your possessions and distribute the proceeds to the poor? If you are, you will have treasure in heaven."

What if? What if Jesus had told the treasure parable to this man and had then asked him, "Suppose you were that man coming upon the hidden treasure. What would you do? Would you do the same thing he did? Would you sell all and buy that field?"

The rich ruler would very likely have said, "Of course I would! Of course I would sell all and buy that field!"

The irony of the situation is that when Jesus stands face to face with the man and tells him in effect, "Do like the man in the treasure parable; go and sell all you have and take possession of the treasure," he does not do it.

Why doesn't he? Because he senses that doing so will revolutionize his life. It will turn all the values by which he has lived so far upside down. And if there is one thing in life people resist doing, it is overhauling their treasured values and rearranging their priorities. Not even a suddenly discovered treasure is worth doing that.

Listening to Jesus' parables is dangerous business. The danger is that we listen to them passively whereas their purpose is to engage us actively. The appropriate question to ask after many of Jesus' parables is, "Is it I, Lord?" The response Jesus' parables call for is similar to the response Jesus called for when he first met Matthew. Matthew was an Internal Revenue officer. One day Jesus passed by his tax office and said, "Follow me!" And Matthew got right up, walked away from his lucrative job, and followed Jesus. In a vague sort of way Matthew realized that the man calling him embodied a treasure that far outweighed in value everything he owned.

Paul

Paul, too, came suddenly upon a treasure—on the road to Damascus. As Paul was going about his business of persecuting the followers of Jesus, the risen Christ suddenly appeared to him. The result of that encounter was that Paul "sold all he had and bought that field."

In his letter to the Philippians, Paul tells us what he "sold" to obtain the treasure called Christ. Paul had many treasured possessions:

circumcised on the eighth day, of the people of Israel, of the tribe of Benjamin, a Hebrew of Hebrews; in regard to the law, a Pharisee; as for zeal, persecuting the church; as for legalistic righteousness, faultless. —Philippians 3:5-6

All of these suddenly lost their value on the day Paul found Christ. Paul writes about this experience,

Whatever was to my profit I now consider loss for the sake of Christ. What is more, I consider everything a loss compared to the surpassing greatness of knowing Christ Jesus my Lord.
—Philippians 3:7-8a

The Ethiopian Eunuch

The Ethiopian eunuch also came suddenly upon a treasure. This eunuch was in charge of the queen's *gaza* (Greek for *treasury*). He was traveling down the road that led from Jerusalem to Gaza.

With this play on words (*gaza,* Gaza) the story of the Ethiopian eunuch invites our attention to the real treasure.

On the road to Gaza the eunuch met the evangelist Philip. Philip joined the eunuch at the precise moment that he was reading Isaiah 53. "Tell me, please," he asked, "who is the prophet talking about, himself or someone else?"

Taking his starting point from Isaiah 53, Philip told the eunuch about the good news of Jesus. Along a lonely desert road, out in the middle of nowhere, the Ethiopian came upon the greatest treasure ever. To lay hold of it, he was willing to be baptized, willing to die with Christ to his old way of life and to be raised with Christ to a new way of life. "Look, here is water. Why shouldn't I be baptized?" the eunuch asked Philip.

Mary of Magdala

Mary of Magdala, too, belongs to those who suddenly came upon a treasure.

In John 20:11 we find her crying outside Jesus' tomb—crying about the death of the man who had cast seven evil spirits out from her.

As she cried, she stooped to look into the tomb and saw two angels in white. "Woman, why are you crying?" they asked her.

Mary answered, "Because I can't do what I came to do—lament over my Lord."

Saying this, she turned around and, through her tears, saw a man that she took to be the gardener. He too asked, "Woman, why are you crying?"

And she answered, "Sir, if you have carried him away, tell me where you have put him, and I will get him."

Instead of answering her, Jesus spoke her name: "Mary." And that voice—a voice she would have known anywhere—rolled the stone away from her sorrowing heart. That voice broke through the wall of her grief and helped Mary recognize her priceless treasure.

The Morality of It

Parables are mundane, secular stories. They relate events that take place in the realm of everyday life: at home, while traveling, on the job. They talk about people who display the full range of human vices and occasionally, like the good Samaritan, some virtues as well. Parable country is home country. Often, however, the parable story contains something out of the ordinary, something that makes the familiar world suddenly look strange and that seems designed to make us sit up and take notice.

In the parable of the hidden treasure, too, there is something unusual, something that makes this story different from the parable that follows—the parable of the merchant in search of fine pearls who, on finding one of great value, went away and sold everything he had and bought it.

These two parables, that of the hidden treasure and that of the fine pearl, are often called twin parables. Though they have their own individuality, it is said, they look exactly alike.

Upon closer examination, however, we find that they are not identical twins, that they are different in at least two respects. For one thing, whereas in the "hidden treasure" parable the man isn't looking for anything at all but is simply going about his daily routine, in the "fine pearl" parable the merchant *is* looking for something.

The second and more fundamental difference is that, unlike the pearl parable the treasure parable reeks of moral compromise and shady business practice. It's a dishonesty cover-up story.

> For what the man does, after all, is to conceal what he has found in order that the owner of the field (and therefore of the unknown treasure) will not know that it is there. If we were dealing with a world in which finders were legally keepers . . . there would be no reason to secure title to the land before walking off with the goods. Instead the man makes sure that the

law is first on his side, in order to make legal a purchase which is unjust.

— Peter S. Hawkins, "Parable Metaphor," in *Christian Scholar's Review,* 1983, Vol. XII, No. 3, 232.

John Dominic Crossan, in his book *Finding Is the First Act* (1979), supports Hawkins' position on the immorality of the purchase. After thorough research in this area Crossan argues against all who defend the legality of the finder's behavior. The question to ask, Crossan says, is the following: Is the treasure ownerless so that the finder becomes the legal and moral owner?

Crossan's answer is this: If the treasure is ownerless and belongs to the finder, why purchase the field? And why purchase it in such haste? If finders are keepers, if the treasure legally belongs to the finder, then this purchase is unnecessary. But if the treasure does *not* belong to the finder—if it in fact belongs to the owner of the land—then purchasing the field is unjust and immoral.

Jewish law, Crossan points out, would have required that the finder divide the treasure with the original owner under such circumstances.

Why does Jesus introduce the element of deception into the parable of the hidden treasure? And what does this tell us about the kingdom?

The parable makes a number of related statements about the kingdom:

First, the kingdom comes to us as a surprise, as a gift, as an act of grace. The man in the parable is not looking for the treasure. He comes upon it unexpectedly.

Second, we discover the kingdom in the course of daily activities. It is not located in the realm beyond death. Nor is it something that will break into our life sometime in the future. Nor does it appear to us in areas specifically designated as "religious." It can appear to us anytime, anywhere.

Third, the kingdom demands total commitment. It requires that we obtain it in exchange for what we treasure most deeply.

Fourth, the kingdom comes despite and through the immoral activities of people such as the man in our parable. Even our best work, even what we sell and sacrifice for the kingdom, is tainted with questionable morality. Upon further thought, isn't the entire history of God's people the story of how God works through people's deceptions and self-aggrandizement to accomplish his purpose? Think of drunken, naked Noah. Think of Abraham lying about Sarah to Pharaoh. Think of what Joseph said to his immoral brothers:

"You intended to harm me, but God intended it for good to accomplish what is now being done, the saving of many lives."   —*Genesis 50:20*

Think of the prostitute Rahab who protected the Israelite spies with a lie, and of Moses the murderer, and of David the adulterer.

God brings his kingdom near just as much through what his servant people do wrong as through what they do right. In the words of Peter S. Hawkins,

God is no respecter of persons, or situations, or presuppositions of how he is to act. Like the preaching of the cross, the parables destroy the wisdom of the wise and bring to nothing the understanding of the prudent. What they offer instead is the sense of living in a world in which anything can happen precisely *because* God is present and working where by all rights he should not be.   —Hawkins, 235

CHAPTER FIVE

The Friend at Midnight

"Suppose one of you has a friend, and he goes to him at midnight and says, 'Friend, lend me three loaves of bread, because a friend of mine on a journey has come to me, and I have nothing to set before him.'
"Then the one inside answers, 'Don't bother me. The door is already locked, and my children are with me in bed. I can't get up and give you anything.' I tell you, though he will not get up and give him the bread because he is a friend, yet because of the man's boldness he will get up and give him everything he needs."
—Luke 11:5-8

Retelling the Parable

In his book *The Parables Then and Now*, A. M. Hunter retells the parable of the friend at midnight in these words:

Late one night a hungry friend turned up unexpectedly at a friend's house and caught him without a scrap of bread in his cupboard . . . . The only thing the householder could do was to wake up a neighbor and ask him for three loaves—the usual meal for one

35

person . . . . Now peep into the single-room house of the sleeping neighbor. His children are bedded in a row on a raised mat, with the parents one at each end, when suddenly at midnight there comes a hammering on the door. The head of the house, startled from his slumbers, is not amused. 'Don't be a confounded nuisance,' he growls to the knocker outside. 'My door was locked long ago. If I get up, I'll disturb the whole family. No, I'm staying where I am—in bed.' But our hero outside in the dark refuses to take 'no' for an answer. He keeps knocking till at last in sheer exasperation the neighbor gets up, unbolts the door, and gives him his three loaves.

When we interpret the parable the way Hunter does, its meaning is both simple and clear: If a human friend can be coaxed into getting up and giving help, how much more likely that God, our heavenly friend, will be willing to help us at any hour?

Rethinking the Parable

Although Hunter's interpretation is a widely accepted one, upon closer examination it proves to contain a number of serious flaws. Hunter exhibits a general insensitivity to the cultural setting of the parable, approaching it with a Western rather than an Eastern mindset.

For example, he views the host as an individual rather than as a member of a larger village community. Also, he sees the three loaves as the usual meal for one person, which they are not. In addition, he misses the meaning of the parable's opening words "Suppose one of you." Finally, he says that the key to the parable is *persistence* rather than *shamelessness*.

A more reliable guide to the meaning of the parable is Kenneth E. Bailey. As someone who lived, taught, and worshiped within the Middle Eastern Arab Christian community for more than thirty years, Bailey's ear is closely attuned to the cultural subtleties of Jesus' parables.

We in the West, Bailey writes, are separated from Jesus' parables by both time and distance. People in the Middle East do not labor under this disadvantage. They very much breathe the same cultural climate as Jesus did.

In his book *Poet and Peasant,* Bailey devotes an entire chapter to the parable of the friend at midnight. We will follow his line of argument closely.

Which of You?

In the Greek original, the parable opens with the words *"Tis ex humon?"* which, literally, means "Who of you?" or "Which of you?" In the gospels, these or similar words regularly begin questions to which the expected answer is: "No One!" or "Everyone!" Following are some examples from the gospel of Luke:

"Which of you fathers, *if your son asks for a fish, will give him a snake instead? Or if he asks for an egg, will give him a scorpion?"*   —Luke 11:11-12
(Anticipated answer: No father will do such a thing!)

"Who of you *by worrying can add a single hour to his life?"*   —Luke 12:25
(Anticipated answer: No one can!)

"Which of you, *having a son or an ox that has fallen into a well, will you not immediately pull him out on a sabbath day?"*   —Luke 14:5 RSV
(Anticipated answer: Everyone will!)

"Which of you, *desiring to build a tower, does not first sit down and count the cost, whether he has enough to complete it?"*
—*Luke 14:28 RSV*
(Anticipated answer: Everyone does!)

"What man of you, *having a hundred sheep, if he has lost one of them, does not leave the ninety-nine in the wilderness, and go after the one which is lost, until he finds it?*   —*Luke 15:4 RSV*
(Anticipated answer: Everyone does!)

In English we would phrase these questions differently. Instead of asking, "Which of you?" or "Who of you?" we would ask, "Can any of you imagine?" "Can any of you imagine having a hundred sheep and, having lost one of them, not leaving the ninety-nine and going after the one which is lost until you find it?" "Absolutely not!" everyone in the audience would say.

Now let's go back to the parable of the friend at midnight. Jesus begins the parable by asking, "Can you imagine having a friend and going to him at midnight and saying to him: 'Friend, lend me three loaves of bread, because a friend of mine on a journey has come to me, and I have nothing to set before him,' and the person inside answering: 'Don't bother me. The door is already locked, and my children are with me in bed. I can't get up and give you anything.' Can you imagine such a thing?"

The anticipated answer to this question, of course, is, "Absolutely not! This is unthinkable!"

Why is it unthinkable? Because the sleeper belongs to a *shame culture*, and in shame culture people who get out of line are shamed back into line. In a shame culture people who violate the community code are held up to public embarrassment.

If the sleeper in Jesus' parable refused the request of his neighbor, his reputation in the village would soon be mud. Good neighbors don't behave that way. Not in our village!

Why Three Loaves?

Why does the host ask for three loaves?

When a guest arrives, Bailey writes, he is given one unbroken loaf. This one loaf is often more than he will eat. Why then give him three loaves? Because Middle Eastern etiquette prescribes that the host serve the guest much more than he can possibly eat.

Where to Go for Bread?

In a Palestinian village there were no bread shops. Bread baking was done daily and cooperatively, and it was generally known in the village who might still have some bread left in the evening.

The host might still have had *some* bread left in his house when the unexpected guest arrived, but etiquette demanded that he offer the visitor unbroken bread. To feed a guest with a partial loaf left over from a previous meal would have been discourteous.

Whose Guest Is the Traveler?

Even though the traveler may have been a friend of the person with whom he was staying, in the eyes of the villagers he was also a guest of the entire village community. The entire village shared in the responsibility for his stay and were determined that the guest leave the village with nothing but praise for the hospitality received.

Two chapters earlier, in Luke 9:51-55, we read of an instance where such community hospitality was refused. Jesus sent his disciples ahead of him to prepare his coming to Samaritan villages. One of these villages refused to receive Jesus. James and John became so furious at that refusal that they asked Jesus' permission to pray God to rain down fire from heaven upon the villagers. They sought revenge not just on the people who actually said no to them but on all of the villagers without exception.

The host in our parable is appealing to his village friend to perform his duty as a member of the village community. His request, then, was not at all unreasonable. In no way did it violate village etiquette. The host did not ask his neighbor to provide him with a full meal. He only asked for what we would call the silverware. For in the Middle East bread is not the real meal. Bread is simply the silverware—that with which the meal is eaten.

Writes Bailey:

Each person has a loaf of bread in front of him. He breaks off a bite-sized piece, dips it into the common dish, and puts the entire 'sop' into his mouth. He then starts with a fresh piece of bread and repeats the process. The common dish is never defiled from the eater's mouth because he begins each bite with a fresh piece of bread.

What About the Rest of the Meal?

The host asks for bread. But he needs more than just bread. He also needs to borrow the common dish—the food that will be eaten with the bread. This is clear from verse 8, which tells us that the sleeper gives the host whatever he needs.

The host might just be at the beginning of a series of stops in the village. From one he asks bread. From another he asks for the main dish. From another, something else.

Nothing?

Why, in Luke 11:6, does the host say, "I have nothing to set before him"? He does so because he is speaking from Eastern culture. He is saying: "I have nothing adequate to serve my guest. If I serve him what I have, the honor of our community will be violated." Again, the appeal to community duty is the main point.

Humor

With this much cultural information as background, the humor of the excuses offered by the sleeper becomes clear. Jesus is saying, "Can you imagine having a friend and going to him with the request to help you entertain a midnight guest, and your friend offering such lame excuses as, 'Sorry, but the door is already locked,' and 'my children are with me in bed'?" To Middle Eastern ears these were ridiculous excuses that were sure to evoke smiles.

Anadeia

A key word in our parable is the Greek word *anadeia* in verse 8. As a quick glance at several translations reveals, this word has generally been translated in two different ways.

New International Version:
"Though he will not get up and give him the bread because he is his friend, yet because of the man's boldness he will get up and give him as much as he needs."

Revised Standard Version:
" . . . yet because of his importunity he will rise and give him whatever he needs."

New English Bible:
" . . . *the very* shamelessness *of the request will make him get up and give him all he needs.*"

Good News Bible:
" . . . *yet he will get up and give you everything you need because you are* not ashamed *to keep on asking.*"

Jerusalem Bible:
" . . . persistence *will be enough to make him get up and give his friend all he wants.*"

One need not know Greek to realize that the Greek word *anadeia* is problematic. Some versions render it as "shamelessness," others as "persistence." But shamelessness and persistence are not the same thing. So which is the correct translation?

Three options present themselves:

The Host Is Shameless

In ancient Greek literature, the word *anadeia* means "shamelessness." The word *anadeia* also carries that meaning in the Septuagint—the pre-Christian translation of the Hebrew Scriptures into the Greek.

The question is this: How does that meaning of *anadeia* fit into the story of our parable? Is it shameless for the host to ask his friend for bread? Is it shameless for the believer to take his or her request to God in prayer?

Certainly not! But that leaves us in an awkward position. If *anadeia* cannot mean "shamelessness," then what does it mean?

The Host Is Persistent

Interpreters of the parable therefore turn their attention to another, but secondary, meaning of the word

anadeia—"persistence."

This translation, too, has problems. For example, where in the parable is the host described as "persistent"? Nowhere! There is not a shred of internal evidence to show that the host is persistent in his request. When he makes his request known to his neighbor, the neighbor answers him immediately.

A. M. Hunter and several other expositors write that the host keeps on knocking until at long last, in anger and frustration, the neighbor gets up and gives the host what he asks for. This, however, is pure fantasy. Nowhere does the parable text support this. The parable contains no record of persistent knocking. In fact, it doesn't mention any knocking at all. What we do read is that the host calls "Friend!" To knock on your neighbor's door at midnight would frighten him. A stranger knocks. A friend calls. When he calls, the neighbor recognizes his voice.

The idea that the host knocked probably came in from verse 9, "Knock and the door will be opened to you."

"Persistence" as a translation of *anadeia,* therefore, won't do.

We are forced to return to the primary and prevalent meaning of *anadeia* as "shamelessness."

The Friend Wishes to Avoid Shame

The crucial question to ask is this: Who is shameless? The host or his neighbor? Most interpreters reply that the host is. But, as we have just seen, this fits neither the parable story nor the cultural setting out of which it arose. The host does not behave shamelessly.

This leaves us with but one choice. The shamelessness attaches to the sleeper. Because of the sleeper's aversion to shame, writes Joachim Jeremias, "that is to say, so that he may not lose face in the matter, he will rise and give him as much as he needs."

The word *anadeia,* Bailey states, is here more appropriately translated "avoidance of shame." Living as he does in a shame culture, the sleeper does not wish to be branded as shameless by his community. His sense of shame tells him that if he does not fulfill his neighbor's request, the villagers will say to him the next morning, "Hey Joseph, what is this we hear? Someone told us you weren't too helpful when Ruben came to you last night!" The implied threat is clear: "We'll remember that. Next time you come to us for help we'll treat you the same way."

Shame is a very powerful weapon in Eastern culture. It is fear of this weapon that makes the sleeper get up and give his friend what he needs.

What Then Is the Kingdom Like?

The parable of the friend at midnight, too, is a kingdom parable. It lights up a certain aspect of God's kingly rule. It tells us something about the King of the kingdom.

When you go to your neighbor at midnight, everything is against you. The hour is too late. Everybody is in bed. The doors are locked. Nevertheless, even with that much against you, you will certainly receive what you ask for. Why? Because your neighbor is a man who will not act shamelessly. He can be trusted to abide by the community code.

The God to whom we pray is similarly reliable. He will not act contrary to his covenant code. He is faithful to his promises. He is not arbitrary, acting this way one day and that way the next. His behavior is consistent with his inner nature. Even though you approach him at the most awkward time, you can count on his helping you.

This interpretation of the parable of a friend at midnight is confirmed by Luke 11:11-13, where the emphasis is not on what *we* are able to accomplish if only we are persistent enough in our prayers, but on the kind of father God is:

"Which of you fathers, if your son asks for a fish, will give him a snake instead? . . . If you then, though you are evil, know how to give good gifts to your children, how much more will your Father in heaven give the Holy Spirit to those who ask him!"

How Then Does the Parable Read?

Can you imagine having a friend and going to him at midnight and saying to him, "Friend, lend me three loaves; for a friend of mine has arrived on a journey, and I have nothing to set before him," and the friend answering you from inside the house, "Don't bother me; the door is shut, and my children are with me in bed; I cannot get up and give you anything." Can you imagine such a thing? I tell you, although he will not get up and give you anything because he is your friend, because of his own aversion to shame—namely, that which will be brought to light through his refusal—he will rise and give you whatever you need.

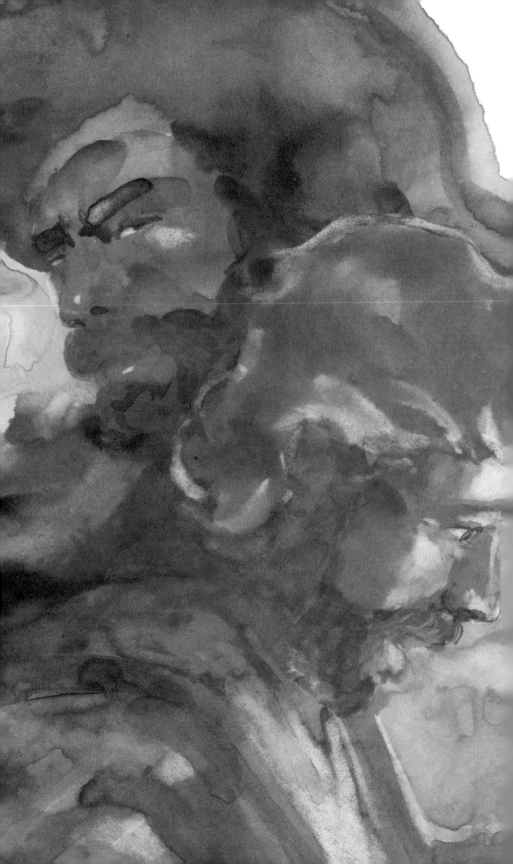

CHAPTER SIX

The Suffering Father

"There was a man who had two sons. The younger one said to his father, 'Father, give me my share of the estate.' So he divided his property between them.

"Not long after that, the younger son got together all he had, set off for a distant country and there squandered his wealth in wild living. After he had spent everything, there was a severe famine in that whole country, and he began to be in need. So he went and hired himself out to a citizen of that country, who sent him to his fields to feed pigs. He longed to fill his stomach with the pods that the pigs were eating, but no one gave him anything.

"When he came to his senses, he said, 'How many of my father's hired men have food to spare, and here I am starving to death! I will set out and go back to my father and say to him: Father, I have sinned against heaven and against you. I am no longer worthy to be called your son; make me like one of your hired men.' So he got up and went to his father.

"But while he was still a long way off, his father saw him and was filled with compassion for him; he ran to his son, threw his arms around him and kissed him.

"The son said to him, 'Father, I have sinned against heaven and against you. I am no longer worthy to be called your son.'

"But the father said to his servants, 'Quick! Bring the best robe and put it on him. Put a ring on his finger and sandals on his feet. Bring the fattened calf and kill it. Let's have a feast and celebrate. For this son of mine was dead and is alive again; he *was lost and is found.' So they began to celebrate.*

"Meanwhile, the older son was in the field. When he came near the house, he heard music and dancing. So he called one of his servants and asked him what was going on. 'Your brother has come,' he replied, 'and your father has killed the fattened calf because he has him back safe and sound.'

"The older brother became angry and refused to go in. So his father went out and pleaded with him. But he answered his father, 'Look! All these years I've been slaving for you and never disobeyed your orders. Yet you never gave me even a young goat so I could celebrate with my friends. But when this son of yours who has squandered your property with prostitutes comes home, you kill the fattened calf for him.'

"'My son,' the father said, 'you are always with me, and everything I have is yours. But we had to celebrate and be glad, because this brother of yours was dead and is alive again; he was lost and is found.'"   —Luke 15:11-32

"There was a man who had two sons." So begins the story that has wrongly been called the parable of the prodigal son or of the lost son. There are two sons in the story, not one. And both are equally lost, the one in a distant country and the other one at home in the midst of his self-righteousness.

The younger son is obviously lost; the older son less obviously. He is what Mark Twain would call "a good man in the worst sense of the word."

Renaming the Parable

"The Parable of the Two Lost Sons" would be a better title for this story. Better, but not good enough—for the

parable is focused not on the sons but on the father. From beginning to end, the father controls the story. The opening sentence reads, "There was a man who had two sons," and the closing verses are words the father addresses to the elder son. So it would be preferable to call this story the "Parable of the Father's Love" (Joachim Jeremias's choice) or the "Parable of the Waiting Father" (Helmut Thielicke). It doesn't really matter which, for the father is waiting because he loves.

Better than any of the titles suggested above, I think, is the one I have used in the title of this chapter: "The Suffering Father." Though the father has been rejected by both sons, he continues to love both and suffers because of it.

The Younger Son's Request

The younger son says, "Father, give me my share of the estate." To Middle Eastern ears this is an unheard of request. A son who makes such a request wants his father dead.

Kenneth Bailey writes that for over fifteen years he has been asking village people all across the Middle East what they think of the younger son's request. The conversation always runs as follows:

"Has anyone ever made such a request in your village?"
"Never!"
"Could anyone ever make such a request?"
"Impossible!"
"If anyone did, what would happen?"
"His father would beat him, of course!"
"Why?"
"This request means--he wants his father to die!"

There is no conclusive evidence that first-century village people reacted the same way to this story as modern village people do. But the fact that the negative response of modern village people is so universal shows that it is of great antiquity.

This is confirmed by Middle Eastern literature. Writes Bailey:

> To my knowledge, in all of Middle Eastern literature (aside from the parable) from ancient times to the present, there is no case of any son, older or younger, asking for his inheritance from a father who is still in good health.

To understand the parable of the suffering father in greater depth, then, we must examine the younger son's request in greater detail. In verse 12, he requests his share of the estate. That share, according to Deuteronomy 21:17, is one third of the property. Law prescribed that if the father granted such a request, the son obtained the right of possession but not of disposition. Even though the younger son now owned the property, therefore, his father still had control over it. Law also prescribed that after the father gave the son his share of the estate, the father still had the right to live off the proceeds as long as he was alive. The father could not sell the property now, having given the right of possession to the son. And the son, because he did not have the right of disposition, could not sell the property and allow the buyer to take possession of it during his father's lifetime.

So the younger son insults his father twice. He launches the first insult when he asks for his share of the estate—for even though the law did not specifically forbid making such a request, a son who made it would break the heart of his Middle Eastern father.

The second insult occurs when the son liquidizes the property that he inherits. The wealth of a village family was held not in cash and treasures but in land and houses and animals. The sudden loss of one third of this wealth meant a great change in prestige and standing to a village family.

Not only does the younger son make a request that social convention regards as extremely heartless, but he also exchanges his part of the family estate for cash. This we may infer from the statement, "Not long after that, the younger son got together all he had, set off for a distant country." This was especially foolish in the Middle East, where negotiations and bargaining sessions take much time and the person who is in a hurry to sell always takes a big loss.

Apparently the younger son doesn't care. He demands and sells his share of the family estate. By doing so he forfeits his real inheritance—his social security and support system. To a villager, family and community are as precious as life itself.

The younger son cuts himself off from these. He wants to be free from his home, free from his father.

Free from the Father

What does being free from the father mean? The Danish writer Soren Kierkegaard answers this question in a story that goes something like this:

> Once upon a time there was a lily growing up in an out-of-the-way place by a rippling brook. Here she lived happily with some other flowers.
>
> Then, one day, a little bird came and visited the lily. The bird

returned again the next day. Then it stayed away for several days before it came again.

This struck the lily as strange behavior. It baffled her to think that anyone could be so fickle, so unattached to the same place.

Now this little bird was a wicked little bird. He made himself important by showing the lily that he was free, that he could come and go as he pleased. He made the lily feel her bondage.

The little bird was not only wicked, but also talkative. He talked fast and loose, true and false, of how in other places there were great numbers of lilies far more beautiful than she. In those places, he told the lily, there was joy, splendid colors, and bird-songs so beautiful that words could not describe them.

So the lily began to feel unhappy and dissatisfied. She felt imprisoned. She now found the murmuring of the brook boring. "Oh," she sighed, "why was I not put in another place? How I wish to become a beautiful lily—perhaps even the most beautiful lily!"

At last the lily took the little bird in her confidence. They agreed that a change of place should be made the next morning. So early the next day the little bird came. With his beak, he pecked away the soil around the lily's roots, so that she might be free. Finished, the bird took the lily under one of his wings and flew away to where beautiful lilies bloomed.

But on the way to the new place, the lily withered. Had she remained where God had put her, she would have been the very lily about whom Jesus once said, "See how the lilies of the field grow . . . I tell you that not even Solomon in all his splendor was dressed like one of these." But now the lily was dead. The little bird had seduced her into thinking that she was not free, that freedom could first be found in a far-off country.

The younger son has the same mistaken notion about freedom as the lily did. Freedom, he thinks, is independence from the father. But the farther and longer away from home he wanders, the more he finds that freedom is dependence upon the father. Freedom is to be found, he finally discovers, in being a son at home with the father.

Going Home

After he has squandered his wealth in wild living, after he hires himself out to do a job that the Torah expressly forbids him to do (Lev. 11:7-8), and after he reaches the point where pig feed looks good to him, the younger son comes to his senses.

Meaning what? Meaning that even though as yet he feels no remorse for the sins he has committed against his father, he is beginning to realize that he has come to the end of his rope.

He is ready to return to his father and offer himself as a hired servant.

As his father's hired servant, he will still be a free man. From his income he will be able to live in the village, independent from his father, independent from the older brother to whom the father signed over everything left in the family estate (Luke 15:12). Living at home would mean having to be reconciled to his brother, a pill too bitter to swallow.

Offering himself as a hired servant to his father, therefore, is the best way out.

It's also the only way out, for as things are now, no one in the village will hire him —not after the way he's treated his father. Not after he's broken up the family estate. Not after he's squandered his share among Gentiles. Upon returning to his native village the younger son can expect nothing but hostility. A mob will gather and throw insults and stones at him.

The father, who knows what will happen when his son returns, runs out to meet the young man as he approaches the village. Running, writes Joachim Jeremias, is "a most unusual and undignified procedure for an aged Oriental, even though he is in such a haste." And Bailey comments, "A man of his age and position *always* walks in a slow, dignified fashion . . . . No villager over the age of thirty ever runs."

Then why does the father run? He runs because he is filled with compassion for his son. He knows how his son will be treated by the villagers. He knows he must get to his son before the villagers do. He wishes to protect the boy from village anger and restore him to his home and community. But to do so, he must humiliate himself in the eyes of the villagers by breaking into a run.

The son never gets to make the proposal he has been rehearsing: "Make me like one of your hired men." The father has something else in mind for him. Rather than have his boy earn back his favor, the father wants him to accept it. When the son says, "I am no longer worthy to be called your son," the father says in effect, "But you *are* my son." And he sends his servants to bring the first robe, a ring, and sandals.

Bailey writes:

The best robe is most certainly the father's. The Oriental listener/reader would immediately assume this. The "first" (i.e., the best) robe would be the robe the father wore on feast days and other grand occasions. The point is that, as guests arrive at the banquet, and as people stream in to see the younger son, to hear his story, and to congratulate him on his return, the father's robe will assure his acceptance by the community. With this command [about the robe] the father assures reconciliation between his son and his servants. At the same time, the father assures the completion of the son's reconciliation to the community.
—*Poet and Peasant,* 185

The ring, in all likelihood, is the family signet ring—the ring with which official documents are signed. It symbolizes that the younger son now has a measure of authority to manage the family estate.

The shoes are also symbolic of his regained status as son. Slaves go barefoot. Sons wear shoes.

Killing the fattened calf means that the village community is invited to celebrate the son's return. Once killed and butchered, the animal is too big to be eaten by just the family and their servants that same day. And if not eaten immediately, the meat will spoil in a couple of hours.

The best robe, the ring, the shoes, the fattened calf—what do all these things mean? They mean that the father is celebrating the restoration of a broken relationship. The father's suffering has not been caused by the lost and squandered part of the family estate. Had that been the case, the son could possibly have made restitution over the years and by so doing have been reinstated. But a new relationship cannot be earned. It can only come as a free gift from the father.

Grace Versus Moralism

With the father saying in effect, "You can never be my servant; you are my son," we have landed in the very heart of the gospel. For the gospel does not say, "If you are sorry enough and humble enough, God will accept you." The gospel says that God's grace always comes first, that coming home to the Father is not an achievement of sorry and humbled sinners, that through the grace of God we already *are* right with God.

But, moralists that we are, we constantly turn things around. We habitually cloud the gospel of grace with a series of "oughts." We think that before the Father will receive us in his favor, we first have to clean up our act and live a better life.

The gospel order is the exact reverse. First, God does something for us. Then we live lives that are shaped by gratitude for what God has done for us.

Moralism is the sin of reversing the order of the gospel. It tells us to start living right. It presents the Christian faith as an achievement. It turns the Bible into a treasure trove full of suggestions for better living.

Moralism corrupts the gospel. People don't become good simply by being told to be good. If they *could* become good, many of them would. The problem is that people are trapped. They cannot do the good they would like to do. What they need is salvation, not moralistic scoldings. These tell us we must first do something for God before He will do something for us, and only lead to frustration and despair. But the Bible says that God's grace always comes first:

"For it is by grace you have been saved, through faith—and this is not from yourselves, it is the gift of God—not by works, so that no one can boast."
—Ephesians 2:8-9

The moralistic younger son says, "I am sorry for what I did, but I will show you by what I will do as a hired laborer that I am worthy of your forgiveness and acceptance."

The father's reply is, "You can never be my servant. You are my son! You may not look like my son, you may not act like my son, and you may not feel like my son, but you are my son!"

The father's love is broader and deeper and higher than the son can ever imagine. He discovers how much his father loves him, how much his father must have suffered during his absence from home. In the face of such love, how can he remain unchanged?

The Older Son

When the party is well under way, when the wine has taken effect and the guests are joyful, the older son returns from the field after a day of hard work. He hears that his younger brother has had the gall to come home again and that his father has welcomed him home. His heart grows bitter, and he refuses to go in.

Custom dictates that on an occasion like this the older son must take charge. He is to greet the guests and make sure everyone has enough to eat and drink. He is also to show joy at his brother's return and to treat him as the guest of honor.

Instead, the older son insults his father by arguing with him while the guests are present. His refusal to participate in a party hosted by his father is an announcement to the village community that he and his father are at odds over the younger son. Writes Bailey,

There is now a break in relationship between the older son and his father that is nearly as radical as the break between the father and the younger son at the beginning of the parable.

For the second time that day, the father offers a public demonstration of his suffering love by pleading with his son. The father could easily tell him off. He could remind him of his social obligations as the older son. But instead he decides to love his older son the same way he loves his younger son.

The father can easily exert his authority. He can easily say, "Now you get in there and do your duty, whether you like it or not. Either that or else." The older son would certainly obey. But what would the father gain? He wants a son, not a servant.

Because he does, the story ends with the younger son inside the house and the older son outside arguing with his father. We are given no solution. We are left with a picture of the father refusing to force his will on his older son and waiting in powerless and suffering love for him to decide to come in.

Gentiles and Jews

Jesus intentionally leaves the story unresolved, involving the listener in the question of whether wholeness will one day be restored to the father's family. Now that the younger son has been welcomed back, the situation has changed for the older son. Will the older son accept the change? Will he join the party? If he does, the father's suffering will be over and the harmony of the family restored.

The harmony of which family? Of the entire human family, if we understand the parable of the suffering father in global terms. The human race, Paul says, consists of two kinds of people: Gentiles and Jews. God's plan for the fullness of time, explains Paul in Romans 11:28-32, is to unite both Gentiles and Jews into the one family of God. God's plan with Israel has not, nor will it ever, come to an end—in spite of their rejection of Jesus, the Messiah. In fact that very rejection, argues Paul in Romans 9-11, is part of God's plan of salvation. "Did God reject his people [Israel]?" Paul asks in Romans 11:1. His answer: "By no means!"

Paul then summons his mostly Gentile readers to stand in awe before the mystery that is Israel. You Gentile Christians, he says, are nothing but honorary Jews, nothing but branches from a wild olive tree grafted into the cultivated olive tree called Israel. It is only by the grace of God that you share in the nourishing saps from the tree called Israel. Apart from Israel you are rootless, cut off from the source of life. Apart from Israel, there can be no church, for the roots of the church lie within Israel.

When Paul tells the Roman Christians to stand in awe before the mystery of Israel, he is telling them to stand in awe before the mystery of God and of his gracious dealing with all people, Jews as well as Gentiles. It's the same mystery that we meet in the parable of the suffering father.

The father in the parable can be seen as God the Father, and his two sons as Israel and the Gentiles.

The older son is Israel. The father pleads with him to accept his younger brother, to live with him in the same house, and to eat with him at the same table.

The younger son is the Gentile Christians. He is challenged to be grateful to his older brother and not, arrogantly, to exalt himself over him.

These are God's two sons, and in Jesus' parable we see how God deals with them: he loves both of them, but he has a hard time getting them to live under the same roof. We see how God does not prefer one over the other, does not disown one in favor of the other. The behavior of the two sons makes the father a suffering father. God suffers just as much on behalf of the older son as he does on behalf of the younger son. He waits for both of them to return to him of their own volition.

This is how God has dealt with us Gentiles. He has prepared a feast for us. "Let's have a feast and celebrate," he said, "for this son of mine was dead and is alive again; he was lost and is found." And the party still goes on.

But Israel, the older son, stands outside and refuses to join the party. The people of Israel refuse to recognize Jesus as their Messiah.

And where is the father? Out in the darkness where his older son boils over with anger and jealousy. Here he shows the same love he earlier showed his younger son. Therefore the parable ends the same way Romans 9-11 ends, with the younger son enjoying food and drink and dancing, and with the suffering father out in the darkness, inviting the older son to join him and his good-for-nothing Gentile brother.

Just as we, the younger son, were once disobedient to God but have now received mercy because of Israel's disobedience, so Israel, the older son, is now disobedient in order that by the same mercy shown to us Gentiles he also may receive mercy. For God has consigned both Gentile and Jew to disobedience that he may have mercy on us both.

CHAPTER SEVEN

The Messianic Banquet

"A certain man was preparing a great banquet and invited many guests. At the time of the banquet he sent his servant to tell those who had been invited, 'Come, for everything is now ready.'

"But they all alike began to make excuses. The first said, 'I have just bought a field, and I must go and see it. Please excuse me.

"Another said, 'I have just bought five yoke of oxen and I'm on my way to try them out. Please excuse me.'

"Still another said, 'I just got married, so I can't come.'

"The servant came back and reported this to his master. Then the owner of the house became angry and ordered his servant, 'Go out quickly into the streets and alleys of the town and bring in the poor, the crippled, the blind and the lame.'

"'Sir,' the servant said 'what you ordered has been done, but there is still room.'

"Then the master told his servant, 'Go out to the roads and country lanes and make them come in, so that my house will be full. I tell you,

not one of those men who were invited
will get a taste of my banquet.'"
—Luke 14:16-24

Far-out Imagery

As measured against ordinary human standards, the kingdom of God is something far-out. To describe it, we need far-out images.

In his book *A Simplicity of Faith,* William Stringfellow does precisely that. "The kingdom," he writes, "may be compared to a circus." And he speaks as one who knows quite a bit about the circus. In the summer of 1966, Stringfellow and a good friend traveled with a circus through New England and part of New York State.

This experience opened his eyes to a number of parallels between the kingdom of God and a circus. For example, like kingdom folk, circus folk are nomadic. They are sojourners who have few possessions to slow them down. Also, like the kingdom, a circus has room for human freaks—for giants, midgets, the excessively obese, Siamese twins, albinos, bearded ladies, fire eaters, and sword swallowers.

In the earliest part of our century, when the circus was in its heyday, such people had few opportunities for employment. The circus was the exception. Like the kingdom, it had room and work for these people.

In Luke 14:16-24, Jesus describes the kingdom in even farther-out imagery. He compares it to a banquet to which God invites the whole world. The boldness of this imagery must have been particularly offensive to the people he addressed—the spiritual elite of Israel. It all takes place when Jesus is invited to dinner by a well-to-do Pharisee. When he gets there, he notices that the guests are choosing the best seats—the ones closest to the host at the head of the table. He then puts this embarrassing question to them: "What if a guest more distinguished than you has been invited to this dinner? Won't your host then say to you, 'Give this man your seat'? Won't that be humiliating? You had better take the lowest place, so that when your host comes he will say to you, 'Friend, move up to a better place.' Then you will be honored in the presence of all your fellow guests."

After giving the *guests* a lesson, Jesus gives the *host* a lesson: "When you give a luncheon or dinner, do not invite your friends, your brothers or relatives, or your rich neighbors."

Why not? Because you're likely to be invited back. You are then operating in the realm of contracts in which you constantly weigh what you give against what you receive. You are then operating in the realm of business rather than the realm of love.

Jesus then says, "When you give a banquet, invite the poor, the crippled, the lame, the blind" (v. 13)

Why? Because they cannot repay you. Because you then have left the realm of business and entered the realm of love, which, if it is genuine, never seeks repayment.

At this point a guest speaks up: "Blessed is the man who will eat at the feast in the kingdom of God" (v. 15). This guest is referring to the great banquet at the end of time, usually called the messianic banquet.

Since this banquet plays an important role in Jesus' parable of the great banquet, we will briefly examine it.

The Messianic Banquet

When the Messiah comes, Isaiah writes, he will invite all the poor and needy in Israel to a free meal:

"Come, all you who are thirsty, come to the waters; and you who have no money, come, buy and eat! Come, buy wine and milk without money and without cost."
—*Isaiah 55:1*

When the Messiah comes to deliver his people and when the messianic banquet is spread, even those who do not belong to God's chosen people—even the Gentiles—will be invited.

"Surely you will summon nations you know not, and nations that do not know you will hasten to you, because of the LORD your God, the Holy One of Israel, for he has endowed you with splendor."
—*Isaiah 55:5*

Isaiah 25:6-9 is even more descriptive of the messianic banquet than the above two passages:

On this mountain the LORD Almighty will prepare a feast of rich food for all peoples, a banquet of aged wine—the best of meats and the finest of wines. On this mountain he will destroy the shroud that enfolds all peoples, the sheet that covers all nations; he will swallow up death forever. The Sovereign LORD will wipe away the tears from all faces; he will remove the disgrace of his people from all the earth. The Lord has spoken. In that day they will say, 'Surely this is our God; we trusted in him, and he saved us. This is the LORD, we trusted in him; let us rejoice and be glad in his salvation."

This beautiful passage pictures salvation as a great banquet to which all peoples—Jews and Gentiles alike—are invited. The days of mourning are over. Sorrow is no more. Death, the last enemy, has been destroyed. Now God invites everybody to the victory celebration.

In Jewish writings from the period between the Old and New Testaments, the vision we find in Isaiah 25 and 55 is dimmed, if not completely lost. For example, the book of Enoch, written about 163 B.C., excludes the Gentiles from the banquet. And one of the Dead Sea Scrolls excludes not only the Gentiles but also Jews who are unrighteous or who have physical defects. The scroll maintains that those who are crippled in either hand or foot, lame or blind, deaf or dumb, senile or of poor eyesight will not be invited to the messianic banquet; they might offend the holy angels.

The writer of the scroll then lays down the seating arrangement for the banquet: The high priest is to sit at the head of the banquet table, then the chief priests, and so on down the line, each according to his status in the religious community.

In that context let's return to Luke 14:15, where one of the guests says to Jesus, "Blessed is the man who will eat at the feast in the kingdom of God." This man has just heard Jesus tell the host that he will be blessed if he invites not people who are able to repay in kind, but those who are not—the poor, the crippled, the lame, and the blind.

By including the very people whom informed theological opinion excludes from the list of invited guests, Jesus cannot but upset his host. Coming to the rescue of the host by attempting to straighten out Jesus' theology, the guest tells Jesus that true blessedness will not come to the poor and the physically handicapped in this present age, but to men of religious status in the coming age.

Jesus responds by telling a parable that can only add fuel to the fire. "A certain man was preparing a great banquet and invited many guests . . . ."

It was important for a host to know how many guests would be coming to a banquet. The number of guests determined what kind of animal and how many of them would be butchered. Writes Kenneth Bailey:

> The decision regarding the kind of meat and the amount is made mostly on the basis of the number of accepted invitations. Once the countdown starts, it cannot be stopped. The appropriate animal is killed and must be eaten that night. The guests who accept the invitation are duty-bound to appear. The host completes his preparations. Then at the "hour of the banquet" a servant is sent out with the traditional message, "Come, all is now ready," meaning the meat is cooked and we are ready for you.
> —*Through Peasant Eyes*, 94

Excuses, Excuses!

At this point in the parable Jesus throws a curveball at his audience: "But they all alike began to make excuses."

These excuses are a rude affront to the host. It's too late for excuses. The animals have been killed; the meat has already been cooked.

The first person to make an excuse says, "I have just bought a field, and I must go and see it. Please excuse me."

This is an outright lie. Bailey writes that no one in the Middle East buys a field without knowing everything about it—whether it has a well, whether it has a stone wall around it, whether there are paths cutting across it, whether there are trees on it, whether there are irrigation problems, who the previous owners were, what profits it yielded during the past couple of years. All these things are checked out before, not after, the field has been purchased. Is the host now to believe that the field has been bought sight unseen?

The second invited guest says, "I have just bought five yoke of oxen, and I'm on my way to try them out. Please excuse me."

This too is an outright lie. People in the Middle East, or for that matter anywhere else in the world, don't buy a team of oxen before they have assured themselves that the two oxen are of relatively equal strength and therefore pull evenly. Not until after they have convinced themselves the oxen are well-matched do they negotiate a price.

The third man says, "I just got married, so I can't come."

This too is a lie. Had he recently married, the groom would not have accepted the original invitation. Moreover, the host would have known about the recent wedding of his social acquaintance and therefore would not have extended an invitation.

By weaving these three transparent lies into his story, Jesus demonstrates his sense of humor. The excuses are so ridiculous that they seem comical. Translated into our time and language, they come across as follows:

> One person has bought a house, but doesn't know where it is. Another person has bought a new car, but hasn't had the chance to drive it. Someone else has married a wife, and she wants him to shampoo the carpet tonight. The excuses, particularly when one considers the

value of property and livestock—
and the subservience of women—in
Near Eastern society, are frivolous,
absurd, nonsensical, insultingly
ridiculous. One can imagine that
everyone is rolling in the aisles with
laughter after Jesus finishes listing
these ridiculous reasons for refusing
the invitation.

—William Willimon,
Sunday Dinner, 56

The Host Responds

Insulted by the declines, the host is
furious. Still, he responds not with
vengeance but with grace. He now invites
the people no one else thinks of
inviting—people whose physical
disabilities are held to be a sign of God's
disfavor and who therefore are
disqualified from attending the messianic
banquet.

Jesus now offends his host by
saying: "The kingdom of God is the exact
opposite of the way you envision it. The
people whom you expect to be there will
be excluded, and those whom you expect
to be excluded will be there. Far from
being an exclusive affair to which only
society's finest are invited, the kingdom of
God is for the dispossessed and the
undeserving."

After the servant fulfills his mission
and the town's marginal people come in,
there is still room. The master then orders
the servant to "go out to the roads and
country lanes" and bring in those from
outside the host's community.

First, the host invites Israel's
religious leaders—those who have the
seating arrangement at the messianic
banquet all figured out. They refuse to
come.

Then the host invites the Jewish
masses, many of whom come and some of
whom still are coming.

Finally, with much room still
available, he invites the Gentiles, many of
whom have come and others who still are
coming. For the parable is open-ended.
The host's order has been issued but
remains unfulfilled as the parable closes.
For anyone who cries out, "Lord, have
mercy on me," there is still room at the
end-time banquet.

As the parable draws to a climax,
the center shifts away from the people first
invited and their reasons for declining, to
the banquet host, who remains the master
of the situation. The people first invited
are strangers to grace and seek to boycott
the banquet by declining the invitation. If
they had succeeded, the host would have
lost control of the situation. But he
remains lord of his original purpose of
filling the banquet hall. The declines he
receives sadden him but do not stop him.
He accomplishes what he set out to
accomplish.

Two Versions Compared

Luke was not the only gospel writer to record the parable of the messianic banquet. Matthew did so too—but with significant differences. To help you see how the Luke and Matthew accounts of the parable differ, we print them below in parallel columns:

MATTHEW 22:1-14	LUKE 14:16-24
"The kingdom of heaven is like a king who prepared a wedding banquet for his son.	*"A certain man was preparing a great banquet and invited many guests.*
"He sent his servants to those who had been invited to the banquet to tell them to come, but they refused to come.	*"At the time of the banquet he sent his servant to tell those who had been invited, 'Come, for everything is now ready.'*
"Then he sent some more servants and said; 'Tell those who have been invited that I have prepared my dinner: My oxen and cattle have been butchered, and everything is ready. Come to the wedding banquet.'	
"But they paid no attention and went off—one to his field,	*"But they all alike began to make excuses. The first said 'I have just bought a field, and I must go and see it. Please excuse me.'*
another to his business.	*"Another said; 'I have just bought five yoke of oxen, and I'm on my way to try them out. Please excuse me.'* *"Still another said, 'I just got married, so I can't come.'*
"The rest seized his servants, mistreated them and killed them.	*"The servant came back and reported this to his master.*
"The king was enraged. He sent his army and destroyed those murderers and burned their city.	*"Then the owner of the house became angry and ordered his servant,*
"Then he said to his servants, 'The wedding banquet is ready, but those I invited did not deserve to come. Go to the street corners and invite to the banquet anyone you find.'	*'Go out quickly into the streets and alleys of the town and bring in the poor, the crippled, the blind, and the lame.'*

"So the servants went out into the streets and gathered all the people they could find, both good and bad, and the wedding hall was filled with guests.

"But when the king came in to see the guests, he noticed a man there who was not wearing wedding clothes. 'Friend,' he asked, 'how did you get in here without wedding clothes?' The man was speechless.

"Then the king told the attendants, 'Tie him hand and foot, and throw him outside, into the darkness, where there will be weeping and gnashing of teeth.'

"For many are invited, but few are chosen."

"'Sir,' the servant said, 'what you ordered has been done, but there is still room.' Then the master told his servant, 'Go out to the roads and country lanes and make them come in, so that my house will be full. I tell you, not one of those men who were invited will get a taste of my banquet.'"

As a quick reading of the two parable versions reveals, there are eight differences between them:

MATTHEW

1. The host is a king.

2. The king invites people to the wedding feast of his son.

3. Two groups of servants are sent out successively.

4. The reasons for the refusal are brief.

5. The second group of servants are treated violently and even killed, whereupon the king in anger sends his army, destroys the murderers and burns their city.

LUKE

1. The host is a certain man, the owner of the house.

2. The man invites people to a great banquet.

3. One servant is sent out once.

4. The reasons for the refusal are lengthy.

5. The servant is not treated violently. Through the host gets angry, there is no mention of a punitive action.

6. The king sends out a third group of servants to the crossroads to invite anybody, whether good and bad.

6. The man sends out his servant twice, once to the streets of the city to bring in the poor, the crippled, the blind, and the lame, and next to the roads and country lanes to make people come in.

7. There is an inspection of the guests. One man is found without a wedding garment and is thrown out.

7. There is no inspection of the guests.

8. The final verse reads, "For many are invited, but few are chosen."

8. The final verse reads, "I tell you, not one of those men who were invited will get a taste of my banquet."

How Do We Explain these Differences?

The answer lies in the different time frame within which Matthew and Luke tell the parable.

Matthew's version offers a sketch of the history of salvation from the time of the Old Testament prophets to the last judgment. The first sending of servants suggests the Old Testament prophets and the rejection of their message (Matt. 22:3). The second sending of servants suggests the missionary activity and the death of the apostles and early Christian missionaries in Jerusalem (Matt. 22:6). The destruction of this city in A.D. 70 by the Roman armies is interpreted as punishment for repeated Jewish rejection of God's invitation.

The sending of servants to the street corners to invite as many as they can find to the banquet suggests the mission to the Gentiles (Matt. 22:9-10). The inspection of the guests in Matthew 22:11 suggests the last judgment, and the darkness suggests hell.

In Luke, the parable's tie-in with salvation history is not as explicit and extensive. Luke's version of the parable also regards the banquet as the messianic banquet—the end-time feast of salvation. But much more clearly than Matthew's version, it offers a vision of the New Testament church as the new messianic community that opens its doors wide to all people. It does not, as Matthew's does, mention the final judgment.

As two ministers may preach on the same text but focus it differently depending on when they preach and to whom, so Matthew and Luke retell the same parable yet focus it differently, Matthew on judgment and Luke on the end-time meal.

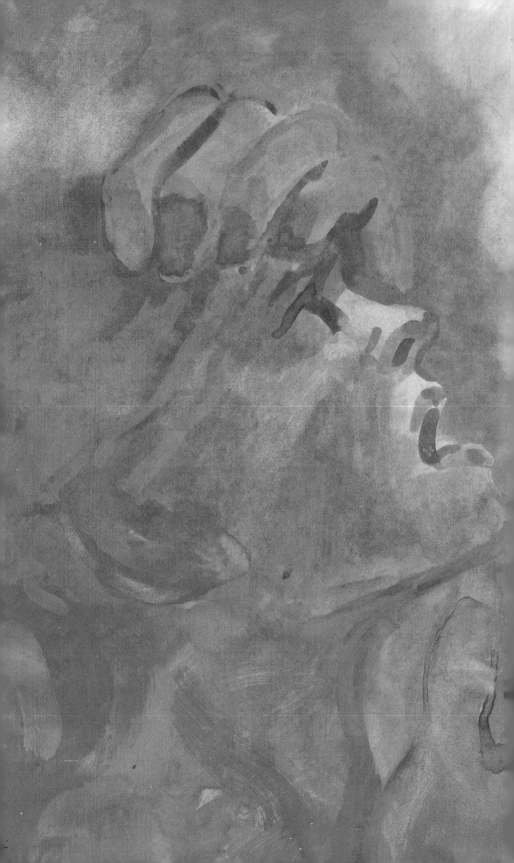

CHAPTER EIGHT

The Rich Man and Lazarus

"There was a rich man who was dressed in purple and fine linen and lived in luxury every day. At his gate was laid a beggar named Lazarus, covered with sores and longing to eat what fell from the rich man's table. Even the dogs came and licked his sores.

"The time came when the beggar died and the angels carried him to Abraham's side. The rich man also died and was buried. In hell, where he was in torment, he looked up and saw Abraham far away, with Lazarus by his side. So he called to him, 'Father Abraham, have pity on me and send Lazarus to dip the tip of his finger in water and cool my tongue, because I am in agony in this fire.'

"But Abraham replied, 'Son, remember that in your lifetime you received your good things, while Lazarus received bad things, but now he is comforted here and you are in agony. And besides all this, between us and you a great chasm has been fixed, so that those who want to go from here to you cannot, nor can anyone cross over from there to us.'

"He answered, 'Then I beg you, father, send Lazarus to my father's house, for I have five brothers. Let him warn them, so that they will not also come to this place of torment.'

"Abraham replied, 'They have Moses and the Prophets; let them listen to them.'

"'No, father Abraham,' he said, 'but if someone from the dead goes to them, they will repent.'

"He said to him, 'If they do not listen to Moses and the Prophets, they will not be convinced even if someone rises from the dead.'" —Luke 16:19-31

Focusing the Parable

The parable of the rich man and Lazarus is about social justice. It's about people who favor tax breaks for the rich and are for balancing the national budget by reducing the amount of public funds allocated for the poor.

In his book *And Jesus Said,* William Barclay claims that this parable is also about heaven and hell. It teaches, he says, three things about life beyond death.

First, it teaches that after death identity remains. After they die, Lazarus is still Lazarus and the rich man is still the person he used to be. The two do not, as many believe, cease to exist as individual persons after death.

Second, Barclay says, the parable teaches that after death memory remains. The story implies that after death the rich man is able to look back over his life and recall, for example, that his five brothers are living contrary to the law and the prophets.

Third, Barclay says, the parable teaches that after death recognition remains. Will a husband recognize his wife? The parable implies that he will.

But do parables provide this kind of information? Does the parable of the rich man and Lazarus offer such information about heaven and hell?

If we say that it does, we lift the parable out of its kingdom equation. We allow it to function independently from the kingdom of God. And, as we saw in chapter 1, this violates the very nature of the parable. The meaning of a parable hinges on being one side of a kingdom equation. Divorced from this kingdom equation, a parable is just a story that has lost its proper focus.

As a parable of the kingdom, the story of the rich man and Lazarus is concerned not with the *world beyond* but with the *here and now* and with the way in which the kingdom breaks into the here and now.

As a parable of the kingdom, the parable of the rich man and Lazarus focuses our eyes on the five brothers. The way they are living leads to death, which is separation from God. The way they should be living, the way of the law and the prophets, leads to life, which is communion with God.

Saying that the parable focuses on the five brothers is but another way of saying that it focuses on us—that we are the five brothers. Like those brothers, we are within calling range of God's Word, and God is waiting for us to obey his voice.

Writes Helmut Thielicke,

> So the theme of the parable which says so much about the beyond is my life and your life. It is as if every spotlight in the house were focused on that spot on the stage where you and I live out our lives . . . the place where we must decide about eternity. And anything that is said here about heaven and hell and the beyond is only the stage setting around this spot on the stage.
> —*Man in God's World, 64ff.*

The Context

The parable of the rich man and Lazarus comes to us in the context of love of money. Luke 16:14 tells us that Jesus addresses this parable to the Pharisees, who are both lovers of money and seeker after pleasure and who bend the Scripture their way.

Now look at Luke 16:18—the verse immediately preceding our parable. It reads,

"Anyone who divorces his wife and marries another woman commits adultery, and the man who marries a divorced woman commits adultery."

What, you wonder, is this verse doing here? How does it tie in with the surrounding verses?

Marriage, Jesus is saying, is meant to be lifelong. We are not free to terminate marriage—even if we find someone better suited to be our spouse. You Pharisees, Jesus points out, twist the Scriptures to suit your pleasure-seeking and money-loving life-style. You cannot justify altering God's ordinances, which never change, to fit your own needs. Where it leads you is away from God. Where it leads you is where it led the rich man in the story I'm about to tell you.

Listen! Once upon a time there was a rich man . . .

An Experiment

This rich man eventually died and went to hell, not because he was rich but because of *how* he was rich. Several times a day he passed by Lazarus, but he never really saw him.

The rich man made the same mistake as the people in John 9 who never really saw the man who was born blind. They saw him only as a familiar spectacle of city life. "Isn't this the same man who used to sit and beg?" they asked. To them the blind man was only a sight. To the disciples he was a fascinating topic of theological discussion: "Rabbi, who sinned, this man or his parents, that he was born blind?" And to the Pharisees the blind man was proof that Jesus was not from God, for Jesus had healed the man on the Sabbath.

Jesus' parable of the rich man and Lazarus is a story about seeing people in need.

By way of imaginary experiment, let's do some supposing. Let's suppose that Lazarus is sitting on the floor in your church sanctuary, in front of the communion table. Let's suppose further that it is dark in the sanctuary so that no one can see him.

You are now in the same position the rich man was in. Lazarus may be sitting right in front of you, but you don't see him.

Now let's suppose you turn on one light—a spotlight that shines on Lazarus. Suddenly you cannot help but see him.

This experiment helps you understand Jesus' parable a little bit better. The rich man does not see Lazarus. Why doesn't he? He doesn't see him because he has turned off all the lights, those lights that shine from Moses and the prophets.

This brings us to the purpose of Jesus' parable. Jesus tells this parable so that we will see people the same way he does, the same way God does. He tells it so that we will see people in the light of Moses and the prophets.

Moses

The word *Moses* is shorthand for the covenant God made with Israel. The so-called five books of Moses (Genesis through Deuteronomy) tell us everything we need to know about that covenant.

The word *Moses* is shorthand for all the covenant laws contained in the first five books of the Old Testament—laws that spell out in great detail what God expects from his covenant partner Israel.

So large is the number and variety of these laws that, at first reading, one may find it rather confusing. But, as Gerhard von Rad reminds us,

this very variety reminds us of the principle that God's righteous will is

to be brought to bear on every aspect of life. There is to be no area, either of public or of private life, over which the sovereign authority of God is not proclaimed.
In relation to every aspect of human life and human activity, God's claim to sovereignty is set forth as the most urgent concern of all.

—*Moses, 49*

The basis of all that God requires of Israel is the Ten Commandments. The many and various laws that follow in the books of Exodus, Leviticus, Numbers, and Deuteronomy are concrete applications of the Ten Commandments to particular cases and situations. When you read them, keep three things in mind: First, these laws lay claim to the entire person. This total claim is most impressively set forth in Deuteronomy 27:15-25:

Cursed is the man who carves an image or casts an idol . . . and sets it up in secret . . . Cursed is the man who dishonors his father and his mother . . . who moves his neighbor's boundary stones . . . who leads the blind astray on the road . . . who withholds justice from the alien, the fatherless or the widow . . . who sleeps with his father's wife . . . with any animal . . . with his sister . . . with his mother-in-law . . . who kills his neighbor secretly . . . who accepts a bribe to kill an innocent person."

What all these prohibitions have in common is that they deal with sin committed in secret. Writes von Rad,

There are many areas of life which the arm of earthly law and justice is too short to reach, or with which perhaps such law is incompetent to deal. But none of these areas

escapes the watchful eyes of God, and the people are called to recognize that He exercises His righteous judgment even over that which is hidden from the eyes of men.   —*Moses, 57 ff*

A second thing to keep in mind is that many of these covenant laws invite God's people to exercise compassion. They show sympathy and consideration for the weak and defenseless. They secure the rights of servants, slaves, captives, widows, orphans, aliens, the maimed, the poor. A good example is the law found in Exodus 22:26-27:

"If you take your neighbor's cloak as a pledge, return it to him by sunset, because his cloak is the only covering he has for his body."

Another example is the law on gleaning in Deuteronomy 24:19:

"When you are harvesting in your field and you overlook a sheaf, do not go back to get it. Leave it for the alien, the fatherless and the widow . . . "

This spirit of compassion extends even to animals, so that the ox treading out the grain cannot be muzzled (Deut 25:4) or a young goat be cooked in its mother's milk (Ex. 23:19). A third thing to keep in mind is that this great variety of covenant laws ought never to be severed from its roots in God's saving action. Israel is called to keep all these laws out of gratitude for God's unmerited grace as displayed in bringing Israel out of the land of Egypt.
The arch-sin of Israel is not breaking this or that particular law, but showing no gratitude to God. Why must Israel have mercy on aliens? Because at

one time Israel itself was an alien and was befriended and redeemed by God. "Do not mistreat an alien or oppress him, for you were aliens in Egypt" (Ex. 22:21).

Why must the rich man have mercy on poor Lazarus? Because at one time Israel itself was poor and hungry, and was fed and cared for by God.

"If there is a poor man among your brothers in any of the towns of the land that the Lord your God is giving you, do not be hardhearted or tightfisted toward your poor brother. Rather be openhanded and freely lend him whatever he needs."
—Deuteronomy 15:7-8

The Prophets

The rich man's behavior toward Lazarus flies in the face not only of what Moses says, but also of what the prophets say. For Moses and the prophets say the same thing: Obey the covenant laws!

Isaiah sums up the central message of Israel's prophets as follows:

Wash and make yourselves clean. Take your evil deeds out of my sight! Stop doing wrong, learn to do right! Seek justice, encourage the oppressed. Defend the cause of the fatherless, plead the cause of the widow. —*Isaiah 1:16-17*

A widely held misconception today is that prophets are predictors of distant future events. It's a view of prophecy popularized by Hal Lindsey through his book *The Late Great Planet Earth* (1970) and through such later prophetic updates as *The 1980s: Countdown to Armageddon* (1980).

Hal Lindsey on the Prophets

Lindsey's end-time scenario, composed of prophetic passages and newspaper clippings, can briefly be summarized as follows: Sometime before the fortieth anniversary of the founding of Israel as a nation—that is, sometime before May 14, 1988—a Jewish prophet will appear in Israel. He will present himself as the Jewish messiah and will lead Israel to sign a treaty with the leader of the European Common Market. This leader is the Antichrist.

> In exchange for the European leader's protection and a guarantee of temple rights in Old Jerusalem, Israel will sign the treaty and worship the Jewish false prophet as the messiah and the anti-Christ as God himself. —*The 1980s, 47*

The state of Israel, says Lindsey, is the center of the events that will lead to the last war of the world.

> Israel is literally the fuse of Armageddon—a prophetic name for the last war. And the Arabs are portrayed as the spark that will light the fuse. —*The 1980s, 53*

The Arabs will attack Israel from the south.

Russia will attack Israel from the north. It will stage an all-out attack on the Middle East in general and on Israel in particular. Russian strategy will be to cut off the supply of Arab oil to the West. To accomplish this, it will first be necessary to destroy Israel, since Israel is the only military power in the Middle East strong enough to resist Russian military power. After double-crossing the Arabs, Russia will be in firm control of the Middle East. Its two remaining enemies will be the Antichrist, heading a ten-nation European army, and the Red Chinese army, boasting around 200 million soldiers. While preparing itself for an attack by these two armies, the Russians will try to destroy the Israeli population. God, however, will intervene and destroy the Russian forces.

With Russia out of the way, only the armies of the Antichrist and Red China will remain to do battle at Armageddon. This last of all wars will be fought during the final three-and-a-half years of world history as we now know it. Armageddon will climax in a holocaust that will wipe out almost all of human life. Only the return of the Messiah, Jesus of Nazareth, will save the world from total destruction. He will destroy the remaining armies, defeat the Antichrist, and establish his millennial kingdom on earth.

In Lindsey's view, prophecy implies future prediction. To him, searching the Scriptures means looking for passages here and there that contain future forecasts. Old Testament prophets, he believes, foretell the far future. They address not only their own contemporaries but the present generation as well. They focus their eyes not on their own day but on our time as well.

By viewing the Old Testament in this way, Lindsey robs the prophetic passages he quotes of their redemptive significance for their own time. He disparages the crisis situations to which they were originally addressed by enlisting them in the service of a bizarre theological construct that does not allow the Old Testament prophets to speak with their own voice.

What Is a Prophet?

What marks an Old Testament prophet is not the ability to foresee coming events but the ability to see the meaning of current events. Insight rather than foresight distinguishes a prophet from the rest of the people. A prophet has the God-given ability to diagnose the terminal illness of his generation—the people's unfaithfulness to their covenant with God.

A prophet is not a humanitarian moved by the plight of the poor. He is not a revolutionary summoning the people to the barricades. He is not a social reformer introducing a new moral order. Rather, he is someone who derives his moral protest from the covenant laws found in the first five books of the Old Testament Scriptures.

A prophet rants and raves because he is certain of two things: (1) God will keep his promise to bless an Israel that lives in obedience to his covenant laws; and (2) God will surrender to destruction an Israel that doesn't.

Future predictions are indeed a part of the prophet's message. But a prophet's predictions are always morally conditioned and therefore can be modified or withdrawn altogether.

Prophets are covenant revivalists. They plead with Israel to embrace anew its covenant with God. They argue that living within the covenant framework gives life and that stepping outside of it leads to death.

Prophets do not merely call for private conversion. They invite Israel as a whole to organize its life around God. They warn that a broken covenant means a broken community, that when people steal, cheat, commit adultery, lie, covet or neglect to care for the poor, human relationships fall to pieces and the nation incurs God's wrath.

The Five Brothers

What Lazarus and the rich man experience after they have died is a polar reversal. In this life the rich man had everything. He was sitting on top of the world while Lazarus sat on the bottom. But after the two men die, their world is turned upside down. The two poles are reversed. The rich man is in hell, and Lazarus is at Abraham's side.

Then, in what appears to be an expression of concern for his five brothers on earth, the rich man says to Abraham: "I have five brothers living just as I did. Please, let Lazarus go back and tell them the outcome of their living."

Abraham replies, "They have Moses and the Prophets. Let them listen to them."

The rich man is simply justifying himself. He is saying that his brothers are living under the handicap of not being warned—just as he did. What he really means is this: "The law and the prophets are not enough. If I had been warned properly, I would have taken care of Lazarus."

But Abraham disagrees. He believes that they are enough. For the law and the prophets clearly teach social justice:

"There should be no poor among you . . . if only you fully obey the Lord your God and are careful to follow all these commands I am giving you today . . . . If there is a poor man among your brothers in any of the towns of the land that the Lord your God is giving you, do not be hardhearted or tightfisted toward your poor brother. Rather be openhanded and freely lend him whatever he needs."
—Deuteronomy 15:4-5, 7-8

CHAPTER NINE

The Compassionate Samaritan

"A man was going down from Jerusalem to Jericho, when he fell into the hands of robbers. They stripped him of his clothes, beat him and went away, leaving him half dead. A priest happened to be going down the same road, and when he saw the man, he passed by on the other side. So too, a Levite, when he came to the place and saw him, passed by on the other side. But a Samaritan, as he traveled, came where the man was; and when he saw him, he took pity on him. He went to him and bandaged his wounds, pouring on oil and wine. Then he put the man on his own donkey, took him to an inn and took care of him. The next day he took out two silver coins and gave them to the innkeeper. 'Look after him,' he said, 'and when I return, I will reimburse you for any extra expense you may have.' "Which of these three do you think was a neighbor to the man who fell into the hands of robbers?" —Luke 10:30-36

There is more than one way to enter a parable. For example, you can enter the parable of the sower by identifying with the sower who looks forward to a rich harvest. But if your life happens to be filled with things that crowd out Jesus, you may identify instead with the thorny soil and examine the parable's interior from that perspective. Or, if you happen to live a rather superficial life, you might see yourself as rocky soil.

Readers, writes Ronald J. Allen, approach a parable at different points in life, in different frames of mind, with different expectations, and tuned to different needs—"all of which may awaken different interpreters to different nuances in the parable" (*Preaching Biblically*, 40).

Thus a rape victim will read the parable of the good Samaritan differently than will the person living in the apartment upstairs who heard screaming but decided to ignore it.

With each approach we enter the parable story from a different direction and become aware of matters that otherwise might have escaped us.

In this chapter we will read the parable of the good Samaritan from two different points of view—that of the original Jewish audience and that of the priest.

From the Point of View of the Jewish Audience

First, we listen to the parable with the ears of the original audience.

Placed in the position of the Jewish audience, we are told that the person who fell into the hands of robbers is "one of us." And our immediate reaction is, "The guy should have known better than to walk down that road all by himself. This seventeen-mile wilderness road has been dangerous as long as we can remember!" When Jesus describes how the priest and the Levite pass by, most of us are not at all surprised. There is enough anti-clerical sentiment among us to expect that much. The priests and Levites among us, however, are deeply offended. They wonder angrily: "Why does Jesus pick on us?"

After the priest and the Levite pass by, we expect a Jewish layman to come along. The temple service, you see, was run by weekly detachments of priests, Levites, and laymen (Joachim Jeremias, *The Parables of Jesus*, 204). Just as delegations of priests and Levites went up to Jerusalem and returned to Jericho after their allotted round of temple duties, so also a delegation of Israelite laymen went up every two weeks to serve with the priests and the Levites. Kenneth Bailey writes:

> After their terms of service, one would naturally expect all three to be on the road returning home. So the listeners note the first and the second and anticipate the third. The sequence is interrupted, however. Much to the shock and amazement

of the audience, the third man along the road is one of the hated Samaritans.
> —*Through Peasant Eyes*, 47

The Samaritan introduces an element of shock into the story, for to the Jews a Samaritan was a social and religious outcast. Though the Samaritans claimed to be descendants from the Hebrew patriarchs (John 4:12), the Jews contested this claim. Samaritans, they said, were racial and religious half-breeds, descendants of intermarriage between Israelites and the Median and Persian colonists who settled in the city of Samaria after it fell in 721 B.C., and who, before long, abandoned their former pagan religions to become indistinguishable from the Israelites among whom they dwelt (2 Kings 17:24-34).

Although the Samaritans recognized the Torah as the word of God and meticulously observed its precepts, this did nothing to alter their exclusion from the Jewish community. The Jews continued to use the Samaritans' mixed racial origin as a pretext for refusing to have any dealings with them (John 4:9). Writes W. O. Oesterley,

> The Samaritans were publicly cursed in the synagogues; and a petition was daily offered to God that the Samaritans might not be partakers of eternal life.
> —*The Gospel—Parables in the Light of Their Jewish Background*, 162

Jews would not permit a Samaritan to touch them, much less minister to them. Accepting aid from a Samaritan, they believed, would delay the redemption of Israel. God, they said, "will bind up our wounds" (Hosea 6:1). How can a

Samaritan act as God's agent of redemption?

Jesus' parable of the good Samaritan forces this question upon its hearers: Who among you would permit himself to be served by a Samaritan? The anticipated answer: Only those who are not in a position to resist such aid. In other words, only those who are truly victims, fully at the mercy of the Samaritan. Only those who understand this are able to understand what the kingdom of God is all about. Only those who have become like the victim on the Jericho road are able to understand what it means to receive God's mercy. The parable of the good Samaritan, writes Robert Funk,

> may be reduced to two propositions: (1) In the kingdom of God mercy comes only to those who have no right to expect it and who cannot resist it when it comes.
> (2) Mercy always comes from the quarter from which one does not and cannot expect it.   —*Semeia* 2, 80

The apostle John sums up the meaning of Jesus' parable in these words:

"We love because he first loved us," and *"This is love: not that we loved God, but that he loved us and sent his Son as an atoning sacrifice for our sins."*
        —*1 John 4:19, 10*

Love, such as God demands we show to our neighbor, does not arise out of our human nature, or out of our religious nature. It does not consist of our imitation of the good Samaritan, or even of Jesus. It is something we cannot create for ourselves at all.

We are, each one, the anonymous victim whom God has made the recipient of his mercy, just as the nameless traveler on the road to Jericho was made the recipient of the Samaritan's mercy. We learn what the love of God is by experiencing his love in our helplessness —just as Paul experienced it on the road to Damascus. He was first God's victim and then, in his total helplessness, became the recipient of God's mercy.

From the Point of View of the Priest

To understand the behavior of the priest, a short story of Bertolt Brecht entitled *The Unseemly Old Lady* is helpful. It's the story of a middle-class woman who, until she was seventy-two years old, always did what people expected of her. She bore her husband seven children. She was an exemplary housewife, being most careful in the way she spent her husband's hard-earned money. She daily cooked meals for a dozen people and always ate the leftovers herself. She never did anything for personal pleasure but strictly limited her activities to her duties as wife, mother, and housewife.

All of this changed when she reached the age of seventy-two and her husband died. From that time on she adopted an entirely new life-style—one that shocked her children. She decided to live all alone in her big house and not have anyone live in with her. She began eating regularly at the town inn. She went to the races. She mortgaged the house, and no one knew what she did with the money. On beautiful summer days she would get up at three o'clock in the morning and walk the empty streets just because she felt like it. She kept company with absolute strangers.

Until the age of seventy-two she had been obedience personified. She had lived solely for her family. Unselfish concern for others had been demanded of her, and she had offered it freely and without complaints. She had met all the expectations placed on her.

But in the last two years of her life a different dimension of her personality began to emerge—one that she had always suppressed. Increasingly she realized how little individuality she had developed during all the years spent in the appointed round of family duties. Suddenly, at the age of seventy-two, she began to see life in a different way. Her love now flowed in channels of her own choosing. While before she had always reacted to the initiative of others, she now chose to befriend a feeble-minded girl. While before she had always skimped and saved, she now bought her friend a hat adorned with roses.

It's easy to criticize this woman's change of behavior. After all, what if all mothers acted as she did? What would become of their families? Aren't assigned positions of selfless service necessary to maintain family life? Bertolt Brecht's story does not answer these questions. It merely seeks to show another dimension of life—one which, because of our culture, often withers and dies on the vine.

Jesus does the same thing in the parable of the good Samaritan. What makes the priest who passes by on the other side behave the way he does? His theology! His ethics! His blind obedience to a prescribed round of duties!

What makes him pass by on the other side is basically the same kind of thing that had previously prevented Brecht's woman from meeting and befriending the feeble-minded girl that needed her so badly. The priest has been taught just whom to love and whom not to love. He is not free to love beyond the barbed-wire fence around his theology. On his way home from serving God in the temple, he suddenly comes upon a dilemma that shows up his theology for what it truly is.

The Middle East, Kenneth Bailey writes, has always been the home of various ethnic-religious communities. Two things tell you who someone is: his speech and his manner of dress. A few quick questions and you can identify someone by his language, dialect, or accent. And a quick glance at someone's clothes will tell you which ethnic group he belongs to.

But what if the person is half-dead? And what if, in addition, the person is stripped? Then how can you tell who he is?

You can't. He may be a Gentile, in which case touching him will make you unclean. He may be dead, in which case touching him will make you ceremonially unclean. And Leviticus 21:1 says that "a priest must not make himself ceremonially unclean for any of his people who die."

The priest is someone who collects, distributes, and lives off tithes. If he defiles himself, however, he can do none of these things, and his family and servants will suffer the consequences with him.

The priest is aware that the process of restoring ceremonial cleanliness is costly and time-consuming. It requires finding and buying a red heifer and reducing it to ashes. It's a ritual that takes a full week.

In other words, the priest is trying to be a good man, but he is doing so as a victim of his theology and as a captive of its many laws. Life for the priest is a series of dos and don'ts, the way it used to be for the old woman in Brecht's story. That which keeps him from reaching out in love is obedience to a theological system.

Such obedience has often crippled the outreach of God's people.

The Inquisition

Think, for example, of what happened during the late Middle Ages. At the same time that magnificent cathedrals were being built in many European cities and that medieval theology reached its peak in the writings of Thomas Aquinas, church leaders officially confirmed the Inquisition that expelled thousands upon thousands of mentally ill people from their homes and communities. Mentally ill people, it was believed in those days, were in league with the devil and had made a contract to obey him rather than the church.

People who served the Inquisition were of the best intentions. Guided by the science of their day, they sincerely sought to heal the mentally ill. Accordingly, they offered prayers for them and with them. If such prayers failed, they used various forms of torture to extract the confession necessary to expel the devil. If that failed, the stake remained the only therapeutic method of snatching people away from destructive demonic powers.

Thousands of mentally ill people—mainly women—were burned at the stake during the Inquisition. They were burned to death because those of the inquisition believed they were acting in obedience to God—just as the priest in Jesus' parable did.

Second World War

To understand the priest of our parable even better, let's bring him into the twentieth century. During World War II thousands of German Christians participated in one way or another in the arrest, transportation, and extermination of six million Jews. They participated because they believed they had no other choice but to obey their government.

Doesn't Paul say that there is no political authority except from God, and that those who exist have been instituted by God? Wasn't Adolf Hitler the lawful authority in Germany? Wasn't resisting him, therefore, the same as resisting God? And so, in the name of obedience to God, thousands of Christians passed by on the other side of Auschwitz.

An Experiment

Still another example is told by Arthur Koestler in his book *Janus* (1978).

A professor at Yale University conducted a series of experiments in the early 1970s. His purpose was to discover how far people could be pushed in obeying authority when told to inflict severe pain on an innocent victim in the interest of a noble cause.

The experiment involved three people: the professor in charge of the experiment, the learner or victim, and the person asked by the professor to act as teacher and to punish the learner each time he gave the wrong answer.

Punishment was by electric shocks of growing severity, administered by the "teacher" on the professor's order. The "learner" or "victim" was strapped into a kind of electric chair, with an electrode attached to his wrist. The "teacher" was seated in front of an impressive shock-generator which had a keyboard of thirty switches, ranging from 15 volts to 450 volts (i.e., a 15 volt increment from one switch to the next).

The entire set-up was purely make-believe. The so-called victim was actually a hired actor, and the shock generator was a dummy. But the teacher did not know this. He was the only one who believed in the severity of the shock that he was told to administer.

The teachers were recruited from all walks of life. They ranged in ages from twenty and fifty and were paid four dollars an hour for their services.

The experiment ran as follows. The victim was asked a series of questions. Each time he or she answered incorrectly, the professor told the teacher to administer a shock and to increase the shock with each additional wrong answer.

As the voltage increased, so did the complaints of the actor-victim, until at 150 the victim cried out, "Get me out of here! I won't be in this experiment any more! I refuse to go on!" Still the professor instructed the teacher to continue to increase the voltage each time the answer was wrong. Finally, after the teacher had administered three shocks of 450 volts each, the professor called off the experiment.

Before the experiment, the Yale professor—Dr. Stanley Milgrim—had asked a group of psychiatrists to predict the outcome. The consensus of the thirty-nine psychiatrists consulted was that

> most subjects would not go beyond 150 volts (i.e., when the victim asks for the first time to be released). They expected that only 4 percent would reach 300 volts, and that only a pathological fringe of about one in a thousand would administer the highest shock on the board.

In actual fact, writes Koestler,

> over 60 per cent of the subjects at Yale continued to obey the professor to the very end—the 450 volt limit.

When the experiment was repeated in Italy, South Africa, and Australia, the percentage of obedient subjects was somewhat higher. In Munich it was 85 percent.

—*Janus*, 85

What the experiment reveals is how little it takes to make people behave like the priest in the parable of the good Samaritan. The boundary line separating good Samaritans from priests and Levites is a very tenuous one. Two-thirds of the teachers crossed it. But for the grace of God, we might very well have found ourselves among their number.

Milgrim's explanation of the cruel behavior of the teachers is not that they acted out of an urge to inflict pain or out of a killer instinct. What the experiment shows, he writes, is that

> the act of shocking the victim does not stem from destructive urges but from the fact that the subjects have become integrated into a social structure and are unable to get out of it.

This, as we observed before, was also the priest's problem. And it is our problem as well.

What this means is that identifying with the priest and walking through the parable in his shoes leads us, the readers, to cry out with the poet of Psalm 130: "If you, O Lord, kept a record of sins, O Lord, who could stand?" Having made that confession, we may then go on to confess: "But with you there is forgiveness."

CHAPTER TEN

The Shrewd Manager

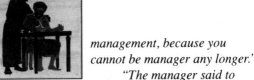

"There was a rich man whose manager was accused of wasting his possessions. So he called him in and asked him, 'What is this I hear about you? Give an account of your management, because you cannot be manager any longer.'

"The manager said to himself, 'What shall I do now? My master is taking away my job. I'm not strong enough to dig, and I'm ashamed to beg—I know what I'll do so that, when I lose my job here, people will welcome me into their houses.'

"So he called in each one of his master's debtors. He asked the first, 'How much do you owe my master?' 'Eight hundred gallons of olive oil,' he replied. "The manager told him, 'Take your bill, sit down quickly, and make it four hundred.'

"Then he asked the second, 'And how much do you owe?' 'A thousand bushels of wheat,' he replied.

"He told him, 'Take your bill and make it eight hundred.'

"The master commended the dishonest manager because he had acted shrewdly." —Luke 16:1-8a

There are some difficult problems connected with this parable, problems that have led many commentators to regard it as the most puzzling of all of Jesus' parables.

One of these problems involves form: Where does the parable end? With verse 7? With verse 8a? Where?

A more serious problem goes right to the heart of content: By using the dishonest dealings of the manager as a model, isn't Jesus compromising with evil? How can he use such a shrewd character to light up the meaning of the kingdom of God?

Where Does the Parable End?

Does the parable end with verse 7—with the words, "He told him, 'Take your bill and make it eight hundred'"? Is verse 8a actually Jesus' commentary on the parable he just told? Should it read, "The master [that is, Jesus] commended the dishonest manager because he acted shrewdly"?

Or does the parable end with verse 8a, showing the master of the parable story commending the shrewd manager?

If "the master" in verse 8 refers to Jesus, then Luke 16:8a is not an integral part of the parable. If, on the other hand, "the master" of verse 8 stands for the rich man of verse 1, then Luke 16:8a *is* an integral part of the parable.

So, does or doesn't verse 8a belong to the original parable? In what follows I will proceed on the assumption that verse 8a is part of the parable. Two strong arguments favor this position: 1. The word *master* found in Luke 16:8 has already occurred twice in the preceding text, once in Luke 16:3 and again in Luke 16:5. In both verses it refers to the manager's master. It is natural to assume therefore that the "master" of verse 8 is not Jesus but the master of the parable story. 2. If the word *master* in verse 8 refers to Jesus, the parable is left without an ending and we don't know how the rich man reacted

to his wasteful manager. Everything is left hanging.

Why Commend the Dishonest Manager?

The second problem is that Jesus seems to be saying, "Let this screwball of a manager be your example." How can such a person serve as a model for kingdom living?

Helmut Thielicke is helpful here. In his book *The Waiting Father*, he reminds us of the sovereign freedom Jesus displays in depicting various aspects of God's kingdom. For example, Jesus compares his Father in heaven with a judge to whom justice is a matter of total indifference and who, in the end, helps the poor widow obtain justice solely because she keeps pestering him day and night.

What God has in common with this hard-hearted judge is not his indifference to justice but his willingness to be moved by people who cry out to him day and night.

Jesus also compares himself to a thief in the night. A thief works under the cover of darkness. He breaks into homes when people are asleep. So, says Jesus, will be the coming of the Son of Man (Matt. 24:42-44).

This does not mean, Thielicke writes,

> that a thief has something divine in him just because our Lord repeatedly said that he—Christ— would come again as a "thief in the night."

The point of the comparison rather is the unexpectedness of the coming.

The argument that Jesus would never have used the dishonest manager as a model for imitation, therefore, does not hold water. What Jesus commends in the manager's behavior is not his dishonesty but his last-minute efforts to save himself before a final reckoning. That and nothing else.

Sequence of Events

The best way to gain a better understanding of the parable of the shrewd manager is by following the development of its story step by step. In doing so I have found Kenneth E. Bailey's book *Poet and Peasant* to be very helpful.

1. Someone reports to the rich man that his manager is wasting his possessions.

2. In all likelihood the manager has been making extra money off his master. But how? By inflating his master's bills? And does he now, after being fired, subtract his "commission" from these bills? Has he been cheating his master by increasing the burden of his master's debtors? The underlying assumption of this line of reasoning is that the book-keeping system is sufficiently loose and the master's auditing system sufficiently sloppy to allow for this form of deception.

Such an assumption, however, is both naive and unrealistic. If such is indeed the case—if the manager has cheated his master's debtors by adding between 20 and 50 percent to the original debt—you can be sure that the manager is deeply hated and that any effort on his part to restore himself to the debtor's graces is simply impossible.

> No further deception, even if it is to their economic advantage, will lead those debtors to welcome him into their homes.
> —*Poet and Peasant*, 89ff.

The manager is a legal agent for his master. As such he receives a fee from his master's debtors. In addition to this legally prescribed fee he will also, as is standard procedure in many countries, receive some money "under the table."

Neither the manager's fee nor the money he receives "under the table," however, is recorded in the manager's accounts.

Bailey writes,

> What is recorded on the bills is known to the master . . . . What is written on the bills is public information discussed openly in the community.

So a manager can cheat in a variety of ways. But if he does, he will make sure that it does not show up on the official accounts. For he must deliver to his master the amounts written on the debtors' bills.

3. The master fires his manager on the spot. This is the bad news. The good news is that he does not have him thrown into jail. By simply firing the manager the master displays a measure of mercy.

4. The manager does some quick thinking. Digging ditches, he thinks, is not for me. Nor is begging. Then a scheme forms in his mind. To carry out this scheme he must act quickly. Until he surrenders the account books, he still has some room to maneuver. Word of his being fired is not yet out, but will be soon.

5. The manager hastily summons all his master's debtors, none of whom knows as yet that the manager has been fired. The manager's scheme will only work as long as they remain uninformed.

Since it isn't harvest time and the amounts of oil and wheat stated on the bills are not yet due, the debtors realize that the manager must have a weighty reason for the summoning. They are not mistaken.

The manager calls them in one by one and reduces their debts, one by 50 percent, another by 20 percent. To the first debtor he says, "Sit down quickly," for time is running out. He must pull off his scheme before the master finds out.

Bailey writes,

> This fact is crucial to the story. As we have seen, the steward was legally powerless from the moment he was notified of his dismissal. If the debtors have any way of knowing that there is deception involved, they will not cooperate.
> —*Poet and Peasant*, 99

6. Since the debtors are still ignorant of the manager's dismissal and therefore think that he is still the agent acting legally on behalf of his master, they naturally assume that the reduction of their debt is legal and above board.

When the manager asks, "How much do you owe my master?" he speaks as though he has not been fired.

The debtors cannot help but wonder, "To whom might we owe this debt reduction? We have not requested one. It's still too early in the season to claim crop failure of some kind or other. There's only one reasonable explanation for this surprise: The manager must have talked his master into it. Isn't he a marvelous fellow! We owe him one!"

7. Having reduced the debts by changing the bills, the manager then turns the changed accounts in to his master.

8. The master looks at the accounts, sees the reductions, and then reflects on his options. He can summon all his debtors and explain to them what transpired before the manager summoned them. He can tell the debtors that what the manager did was illegal. He can then reinstate the original debts.

But if he were to do so, he would be cursed up and down by the entire community. The debtors by now have returned home and have told their family and friends. They may already have started a celebration in praise of their generous master and his sympathetic manager. Wine may already be flowing. For him to spoil this celebration would ruin his reputation.

This brings us to the second choice the master has. He can accept the praise of the community and allow his manager, who supposedly talked his master into it, to bathe in popularity. This, the master realizes, is his only realistic option. For his reputation in the community is of far greater value than the 400 gallons of olive oil and the 200 bushels of wheat out of which his manager has bamboozled him.

The master reflects for a moment and concludes that his manager has outsmarted him and that, realistically speaking, he has only one choice—to leave things the way they are and accept people's praise for his generosity. "Clever fellow! Clever fellow!" he mumbles under his breath. Then he turns to his former manager and tells him so.

The Meaning of the Parable

The manager, scoundrel though he is, at least makes a realistic assessment of the crisis he is in. He draws up a clever plan to ward off economic disaster and manages to pull it off.

Jesus does not commend the dishonesty of the manager who feathered his future nest by making his master's debtors indebted to him. What Jesus commends him for is his resourcefulness.

As originally told, the parable has an eschatological meaning: it calls the listeners to prepare for the last (Greek: *eschatos*) crisis—the coming of the Son of Man. Just as the manager, confronted by a life-threatening situation, considers his options and chooses the one that offers him the best possible future, so we ought to make an appropriate response to the crisis in which Jesus' preaching of the kingdom of God places us. We are to think as boldly and act as decisively as the manager did.

Writes Herman Hendrickx,

Luke 16:1-8a is, therefore, a crisis parable. It is the steward's ability to deal with a crisis which is the point of the story, the reason for the master's commendation, and the example for the disciples. This is the message of the original parable.
—*The Parables of Jesus*, 192

Appended Sermon Notes

Appended to the parable of the shrewd manager are a number of Jesus' sayings. These sayings show how the early Christian community applied this parable to their situation.

Just as your pastor may preach on the same text more than once but approach and apply it differently each time, so the early Christian community approached and applied Jesus' parables differently at different times.

In Luke 16:8b-13 we almost can see, as one commentator puts it, notes for three separate sermons on the parable of the shrewd manager:

1. "I tell you, use worldly wealth to gain friends for yourselves, so that when it is gone, you will be welcomed into eternal dwellings."   —*Luke 16:9*

Of the three appended applications, this one is most in line with the original intent of Jesus' parable. If the dishonest manager provides for his future by an improper use of possessions, how much more should Christians, through proper use of money, provide for their eternal future.

Blessed are those who share their wealth with the poor, for theirs is the kingdom of heaven.

2. "Whoever can be trusted with very little, can also be trusted with much, and whoever is dishonest with very little will also be dishonest with much. So if you have not been trustworthy in handling worldly wealth, who will trust you with true riches? And if you have not been trustworthy with someone else's property, who will give you property of your own?"
—*Luke 16:10-12*

These words of Jesus, too, are a commentary on the parable of the dishonest manager. If Christians aren't faithful in using the little money they have, these verses imply, how can they be trusted with "true riches"—the riches of the kingdom of God?

The story of the widow's offering comes to mind. Jesus sits opposite the temple treasury, watching people drop money into the chest. He observes how many rich people throw in large amounts and how a poor widow puts in two very small copper coins. He comments to his disciples:

"This poor widow has put more into the treasury than all the others. They gave out of their wealth; but she, out of her poverty, put in everything—all she had to live on."
—*Mark 12:43-44*

3. "No servant can serve two masters. Either he will hate the one and love the other, or he will be devoted to the one and despise the other. You cannot serve both God and Money."—Luke 16:13

There is, Jesus is saying, a direct relationship between money and the kingdom of God. Tell me how you spend your money and I will tell you whether you're in the kingdom or not.

Each of the above three applications is a proper commentary on the parable of the shrewd manager. Each challenges us to react radically to the crisis in which the preaching of the kingdom of God places us. We are to think as boldly and to act as decisively as the dishonest manager did.

CHAPTER ELEVEN

The Pharisee and the Tax Collector

"Two men went up to the temple to pray, one a Pharisee and the other a tax collector. The Pharisee stood up and prayed about himself: 'God, I thank you that I am not like other men—robbers, evildoers, adulterers—or even like this tax collector. I fast twice a week and give a tenth of all I get.'

"But the tax collector stood at a distance. He would not even look up to heaven, but beat his breast and said, 'God, have mercy on me, a sinner.'

"I tell you that this man, rather than the other, went home justified before God." —Luke 18:10-14

The parable of the Pharisee and the tax collector is about seeing. It's about how we see ourselves, how we see others, and how God sees us.

How We See

There is a widespread misconception that the parable of the Pharisee and the tax collector presents us with two models—one to be imitated, the other to be ignored. According to this interpretation, the Pharisee models the proud and pious believer, the tax collector the humble and repentant sinner.

To read the parable in this fashion is to read it in black and white, as one Sunday School teacher did. "Children," the teacher informed his class, "this parable teaches us that we should thank God that we are not like that Pharisee."

A parable is a trap. Once you're in it, you can't get out. No door allows you to exit. So, upon reading the parable of the Pharisee and the tax collector, you're stuck with both men. You can't say, "The tax collector is my model," and then proceed to ignore the Pharisee. With no door through which to exit from the parable, you are forced to deal with the Pharisee as well. You have no choice but to come to know both men, until finally you have to admit that you are more like the Pharisee than the tax collector, or until you realize that you are a cross between the two men, perhaps one who prays like this:

> I thank you, God, that I am not so proud as this Pharisee; I am an extortioner, unjust, and an adulterer. That's the way human beings are, and that's what I am, but at least I admit it. That makes me a little better than the rest of the breed. I commit fornication twice a week, and at most ten percent of what I own comes from honest work. I am an honest man, O God, because I don't kid myself, I don't have any illusions about myself. Let your angels sing a hallelujah over this one sinner who is as honest as I am, honest enough to admit that he is a dirty dog. Honest enough not to hide it beneath his robes like these lying Philistines the Pharisees.
>
> —Helmut Thielicke,
> *The Waiting Father*, 129

Because we tend to read this parable moralistically, looking for a model to imitate, we have gotten rid of the Pharisee too fast and too often. How many times haven't preachers told us to imitate the tax collector and disown the Pharisee? How often haven't our teachers condemned the self-righteousness of the Pharisee and praised the honesty and humility of the tax collector?

If only things were that simple! But a parable is a trap. It forces us to recognize, more often later than sooner, that we are Pharisee and tax collector wrapped into one and that we constantly change over from one into the other.

To illustrate this point, all we have to do is run a quick check on those characters in Jesus' parables with whom we tend to identify.

We identify with the prodigal son rather than with his disgruntled older brother. We identify with the people who accept the invitation to the great banquet rather than with those who make excuses and stay home. Similarly we identify with the tax collector rather than with the Pharisee.

By doing so we moralize Jesus' parables. We choose the character whom we feel is worthy of imitation and refuse to deal with the undesirable characters. We choose the side in us with which we can cope and refuse to confront our dark and disagreeable side.

How Jesus' Contemporaries Saw

Jesus' contemporaries saw the Pharisee and the tax collector quite differently than we do. If they had seen them as we do, Jesus wouldn't have bothered to tell this parable. If the Pharisee was indeed the arrogant and sanctimonious person we have stereotyped him as, and if the tax collector was indeed the deeply humble and repentant person we have been led to think he was, what possible reason might Jesus have had for telling the people what to them was so obvious? "But of course!" they would have said after Jesus had told the parable. "Obviously the tax collector went home justified before God!"

But to Jesus' contemporaries the conclusion of the parable came as a shock. Unquestionably they had expected Jesus to say that the Pharisee went home justified before God.

Why did the people expect this kind of ending? To find out, let us follow the flow of the parable story.

"Two men went up to the temple to pray . . ."

Traditionally we have understood these words to mean that each of these men went up to the temple to engage in private prayer. But, as Kenneth E. Bailey points out, this is due to our individualistic (Western) way of reading Jesus' parables. Middle Easterners read the parable of the Pharisee and the tax collector and instinctively assume that it talks about public worship.

Bailey points to five pieces of evidence in the parable showing that the Middle Eastern way of reading is right and ours wrong:

1. Two people go up to a place of *public* worship at the *same* time.

2. They go home at the *same* time, presumably after the temple service is over.

3. The temple—a place of public worship—is specifically mentioned.

4. The tax collector stands "at a distance." At a distance from whom? From the Pharisee? Possibly! Or at a distance from the rest of the worshipers? More likely!

5. In his prayer, the tax collector asks God to have mercy on him, a sinner. In other words, the substance of his prayer is the atonement. The temple ritual included a daily morning and evening atoning sacrifice. At these sacrifices a congregation was normally present.

In view of these five pieces of evidence, it is safer to assume that the parable pictures two men going up to the temple to engage in public rather than in private worship.

In Jesus' day there were two daily temple services, one at 9 A.M. and one at 3 P.M. Worshipers would draw near to the altar on which a lamb was being sacrificed to atone for the sins of Israel. After the

sacrifice ritual, the officiating priest would leave the altar and enter the Holy Place. Upon fulfilling his duties there, he would return to the altar.

During the priest's absence from the altar, the people would offer private prayers—the kind we hear the Pharisee and the tax collector offer. The sacrifice of the lamb on the altar had covered the sins of Israel and had opened the way to God. Now the people could freely offer prayers.

"Two men went up to the temple to pray, one a Pharisee and the other a tax collector."

The Pharisee stands up and prays about himself. He first lists the sins from which he has refrained: "God, I thank you that I am not like all other men—robbers, evildoers, adulterers—or even like this tax collector." He then lists his good deeds: "I fast twice a week and give a tenth of all I get."

He offers God both his person and his purse. He does everything his religion demands of him and even more. There's no question about it. He is a very good man.

The Pharisee has often been rapped for his self-congratulatory attitude, for the way he assumes that he is righteous before God whereas the tax collector is not.

But look again. His prayer begins with, "God, I thank you . . ." He recognizes that he is what he is by the grace of God, that his goodness is a gift of God, and that God has kept him from falling into the kind of sins he sees the tax collector committing.

Nor does he ask God for anything. His only goal is thanksgiving.

Joachim Jeremias tells us that a similar prayer has come down to us from the first century A.D. in the Talmud—the authoritative collection of Jewish tradition. This prayer reads:

I thank thee, O Lord, that thou hast given me my lot with those who sit in the seat of learning, and not with those who sit at the street-corners; for I am early to work, and they are early to work; I am early to work on the words of the Torah [i.e., the first five books of the Old Testament], and they are early to work on things of no moment. I weary myself, and they weary themselves; I weary myself and profit thereby, while they weary themselves to no profit. I run and they run; I run towards the life of the Age to Come, and they run towards the pit of destruction.

—Joachim Jeremias, *The Parables of Jesus*, 142

So evidently the Pharisee's prayer in Jesus' parable is taken from real life and is not just something Jesus composes to heighten the effect of his parable.

How God Sees

What's wrong with the Pharisee's prayer? The comparisons it makes: "I am not like other men—robbers, evildoers, adulterers—or even like this tax collector."

What's wrong with this prayer is the spirit of pride it breathes, for pride thrives on comparison. Pride is not like other sins. Pride, C. S. Lewis says, is the great sin, the mother sin, the sin that gives birth to all other sins.

Pride, Lewis writes,

is *essentially* competitive—is competitive by its very nature—while the other vices are competitive only, so to speak, by accident. Pride gets no pleasure out of having something, only out of having more of it than the next man.

We say that people are proud of being rich, or clever, or good-looking, but they are not. They are proud of being richer, or cleverer, or better-looking than others. If everyone became equally rich, or clever, or good-looking, there would be nothing to be proud about. It is the comparison that makes you proud: the pleasure of being above the rest.

—*Mere Christianity*, 109-110

If you wish to know yourself, you need a standard against which to measure yourself. The Pharisee measures himself against the tax collector and comes out smelling like a rose. Surely, the Pharisee knows himself well enough to realize that all is not well with him, that there are rats living in his basement, that frightful thoughts and desires constantly come bubbling up from the depths of his heart to the surface of his consciousness. But, he thinks, I know how to deal with them. I know how to control them while the tax collector doesn't.

The Pharisee draws comparisons between himself and the tax collector. Anybody doing this is bound to become proud. The tax collector draws no such comparisons. Rather, he measures himself against God and realizes that in God's presence all is grace, that in God's presence it makes no difference how moral or immoral you are, since both the moral and the immoral depend on the mercy of God.

Flannery O'Connor's short story *Revelation* focuses precisely on that point. In this story a certain Mrs. Turpin sits in a doctor's waiting room judging the acceptable and unacceptable people around her. She approves of her own kind and dismisses all the others as "white-trash" or "niggers."

On sleepless nights Mrs. Turpin had often reflected on the question of

who she would have chosen to be if she couldn't have been herself. If Jesus had said to her before he made her, "There's only two places available for you. You can either be a nigger or white-trash," what would she have said? "Please, Jesus, please," she would have said, "just let me wait until there's another place available."

When Mrs. Turpin thinks of all she might have been besides herself, she just feels like shouting "Thank you, Jesus, for making everything the way it is!"

Later in the day she returns to the farm and goes about her chores. In the glow of the setting sun, she has a vision of a bridge swinging from earth to heaven. Walking on that bridge is a large crowd of people making their way to heaven. The crowd is made up of all those types of people that Mrs. Turpin has passed judgment on at the doctor's office. It's a crowd made up of white-trash, "clean for the first time in their lives," and black niggers dressed in white robes, and "battalions of freaks and lunatics shouting and clapping and leaping like frogs." And the rear of the procession is made up of people like Mrs. Turpin.

Looking carefully at these people, people like herself, Mrs. Turpin can see by their shocked and changed faces that all their virtues are being burned away. The last have become first and the first have become last. The tax collector has become first and the Pharisee has become last.

The Pharisee's prayer sounds a lot like the beginning of Psalm 26:

Vindicate me, O Lord, for I have led a blameless life; I have trusted in the Lord

without wavering. Test me, O Lord, and try me, examine my heart and my mind; for your love is ever before me, and I walk continually in your truth. I do not sit with deceitful men, nor do I consort with hypocrites; I abhor the assembly of evildoers and refuse to sit with the wicked. I wash my hands in innocence, and go about your altar, O Lord, proclaiming aloud your praise and telling of all your wonderful deeds.

The psalmist seems to be saying much the same thing as the Pharisee says: "I don't do this and I don't do that. I don't hang around with bad and phony guys. I live a blameless life and trust in the Lord."

Where the Pharisee's prayer differs is that it leaves out the final petition of Psalm 26: "redeem me and be merciful to me."

The Pharisee thinks of God as a bookkeeper. The psalmist thinks of God as his merciful redeemer. The Pharisee thinks he can make himself acceptable to God by what he does. The psalmist believes that God does not work that way, that God loves us regardless of what we do.

How We Must See

The Pharisee and the tax collector. A few of us are one or the other all the time. Most of us are some of both much of the time.

There are times when we are Pharisees, when our sincere prayer changes over into self-congratulation, when our well-intentioned prayer turns in upon itself so that it is difficult to tell if it is addressed to God or to ourselves. We do not feel the need for God's mercy and we receive none.

There are also times when we come before God as tax collectors, when we need everything and go home with more than we dared ask for.

Jesus does not say that the tax collector in us is more upright than the Pharisee in us. On the contrary. The tax collector's condition is so wretched and his future so void of hope that he is not someone to admire or imitate. There is nothing left for the tax collector but to pray: "*Kyrie eleison*! Lord, have mercy! Lord, let the atonement sacrifice be for me!"

And when, stripped bare of the things we like to show God, we go back home justified, it is not because we prayed correctly or because we struck a humble enough pose, for God owes us nothing. The only reason we go home justified is because God is merciful.

Picture an old European village and in the center of it a church with a tall tower. Around the church are small houses, a tavern, some shops.

Standing in the village square, you see someone come out of church, Bible in hand. Then you see someone else stagger out of the tavern, dead-drunk. And you think, "What a difference!"

But climb the tall church tower, one endless flight of steps after the other. Then look down on the village square, and all the differences you observed below have disappeared. From where you are standing now, you no longer see whether people are sober or drunk, church-goers or tavern-goers. All you see are tiny figures, one indistinguishable from the other.

That's the way God sees us. In God's eyes we're all the same: mixtures of Pharisee and tax collector, all equally in need of his mercy.

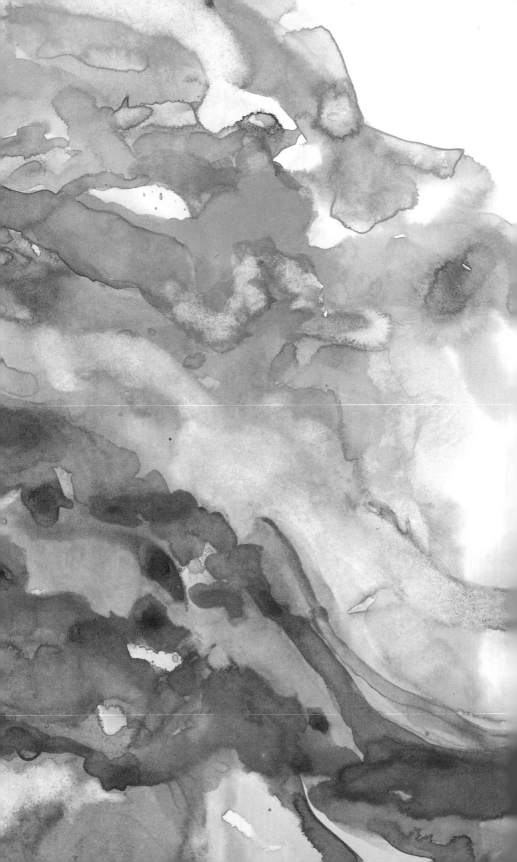

CHAPTER TWELVE

Jesus as Parable

Jesus' parables, we learned in chapter 2, proclaim the kingdom of God. But so does Jesus' life. Jesus' life as a whole, including his death and resurrection, proclaims the kingly rule of God. The life story of Jesus discloses to us a new world, a new way of being in the world, a new way of living that is marked by total submission to the rule of God.

So Jesus is more than a teller of parables. *He himself is a parable.* Or rather, he is the definitive parable. Jesus *is* what he proclaims. At the same time he is both proclaimer and proclamation of God's kingly rule.

Jesus as Parable

In what sense can Jesus be called a parable?

In his provocative article, "Jesus, the Parable of God," Leander Keck calls our attention to the following parallels:

Parables Are Clean Windows

Clean windows invite us not to look *at* them, but to look *through* them. Jesus' parables do the same. They offer us a view of God's world beyond the parable story. They don't look at the everyday world we meet in the parable story; they look through this world to offer us glimpses of the world where God's name is hallowed and his will is done.

What Jesus' parables seek to do may be illustrated by Franz Kafka's modern parable "Give It Up":

It was very early in the morning, the streets clean and deserted. I was on my way to the

95

station. As I compared the tower clock with my watch, I realized it was much later than I had thought and that I had to hurry. The shock of this discovery made me feel uncertain of the way. I wasn't very well acquainted with the town as yet; fortunately, there was a policeman at hand. I ran up to him and breathlessly asked him the way. He smiled and said: "You are asking me the way?" "Yes," I said, "since I can't find it myself."

"Give it up! Give it up!" said he, and turned with a sudden jerk, like someone who wants to be alone with his laughter.

Upon first reading, Kafka's story strikes us as totally absurd. The outcome of the story doesn't make any sense. It completely violates the rules by which we live.

As the person who is hurrying to the station becomes disoriented and then in desperation turns to the policeman, we feel confident that the policeman will give him directions. When it comes to finding the way around town, he is the person to ask. If *he* doesn't know where the station is, who does?

The policeman's answer comes as a complete shock. His answer "Give it up! Give it up!" totally abolishes the realism of the story. It opens the door to an entirely different world—a world ruled by alien values.

Kafka's parable helps us to understand Jesus' parables. It helps us to understand the strange world they disclose, the world in which all of our conventional values are turned upside down.

We are now in a position to understand why Jesus can be called a parable. In order for us to see what God's

kingly rule is like—something strange and unfamiliar about which we do not know how to think or talk—we must look through Jesus.

Like a clean window, Jesus does not attract attention to himself but to the kingdom he proclaims. He is not impressed with his own importance but is rather the human transparency through which we can view God's kingly rule.

Jesus is the only clean window offering such a view. When a person looks at me, Jesus says in John 12:45, "he sees the one who sent me." Just as from the inside of our living room we can see the outside world only through the living room window, so, from the inside of our life, we can see God's world only through the window which is Jesus.

Parables Are Total Comparisons

A parable does not make a partial comparison; it makes a total comparison. This distinction is crucial for understanding Jesus' parables and Jesus as parable.

When I say that Harry smokes *like* a chimney, I make a partial comparison. I merely offer a side view of Harry. Harry may smoke like a chimney, but he may also play tennis like a pro and treat his employees like a father.

A parable doesn't make this kind of partial comparison. Instead it draws a total comparison that can be very shocking or damning. For example, when I say that Harry *is* a smoking chimney, I am saying a lot more than when I say that he is *like* a smoking chimney. When I say he *is* a smoking chimney, I'm saying that smoking controls his entire life, that the first thing Harry does when he gets up in the morning is light up and that the last thing he does before he goes to bed is smoke one more cigarette.

Similarly, when Jesus says that King Herod *is* a fox, he is not offering a partial description of that monarch. He is characterizing Herod as a whole, so that people who hear Jesus are forced to revise their total image of Herod. By telling us that Herod is a fox, Jesus sets the total Herod before our eyes.

It is in this sense—this total sense—that Jesus can be called a parable. For it is the totality of Jesus—his words, his thoughts, his life, his ministry, his death, his resurrection—that shows forth the kingly rule of God.

When we describe Jesus as parable, we are not saying that his life *illustrates* the kingdom of God. A parable, we learned in chapter 1, is not an illustration. It does not illustrate what can better be stated in non-parabolic language. It says what cannot be said in any better way. A parable is the main meal, not an appetizer. It is the main story, not an illustration.

Accordingly, when we characterize Jesus as parable, we are saying that the whole of Jesus embodies the kingdom. We are saying that in Jesus the kingdom became flesh.

As the definitive parable, Jesus invites us to see the kingdom of God through him because we cannot see it through anyone else. Access to the kingdom is gained exclusively through him. To submit to the authority of God is tantamount to submitting to Jesus. Conversely, to submit to Jesus is tantamount to submitting to the rule of God as revealed in Jesus.

Parables Are Topsy-Turvy Stories

Whereas some of Jesus' parables portray typical, true-to-life situations, many of them do not. Most parables portray atypical, bizarre, unconventional, or outright shocking situations.

For example, it is hardly typical for a merchant to sell everything in order to buy a single pearl. The average merchant is cautious, not likely to put all his eggs in one basket.

Nor is it typical for a Middle Eastern father to run, as we saw him do in chapter 6. To run is undignified and humiliating.

Nor is it typical for the owner of a vineyard to pay equal wages to laborers whom he has hired at different hours of the day, or for every invited guest to refuse a banquet invitation at the last minute.

A parable like that of the Messianic Banquet (see chapter 7) stretches our sense of reality to the breaking point. All those who have been invited decline the invitation for what are sham excuses: "I have just bought a field, and I must go and see it" (But no one in the Middle East buys land sight unseen); "I have just bought five yoke of oxen, and I'm on my way to try them out" (But trying out is always done before the buying); "I just got married, so I can't come" (But if there had been a wedding in the village that same day, the host would have known about it and have scheduled his banquet for another day). All three excuses are phony, and everyone knows they are.

Then, after rounding up the poor, the crippled, the blind, and the lame from the streets, Jesus turns to the roads and country lanes, and the crowd becomes a horde.

At this point the parable story assumes absurd proportions. Obviously, no home is big enough to accommodate that many people. The capacity of the banquet hall appears limitless. So does the host's supply of china and silverware.

The question is this: Why does Jesus distort reality in his parables? What point is he making?

This point: In the world of God's kingdom things are the opposite of what they are in our world. As measured by the standards of our world, God's world is topsy-turvy.

Jesus' parables compel us to compare our world with God's world. They juxtapose our dog-eat-dog world, where the prime values are self-fulfillment, self-preservation, and security, with God's world, where the weak are cherished, the poor are blessed, and the last are first.

The topsy-turviness of Jesus' parables makes them shocking stories. Similarly, the topsy-turviness of Jesus' life makes it a shocking life. Jesus not only tells shocking stories, he also leads a shocking life and dies a shocking death.

The gospel writer Mark saw this clearly. Between chapters 2:1 and 3:5 Mark brings together five shocking stories:

1. The healing of a paralytic whose sins Jesus forgives
(Reaction: "He's blaspheming! Who can forgive sins but God alone?")

2. A meal Jesus shares with marginal people
(Reaction: "Why does he eat with tax collectors and 'sinners'?")

3. Jesus' defense of his disciples for not fasting
(Reaction: "How is it that John's disciples and the disciples of the Pharisees are fasting, but yours are not?")

4. Jesus' defense of his disciples for picking some heads of grain
(Reaction: "Look, why are they doing what is unlawful on the Sabbath?")

5. Jesus' healing on the Sabbath of a man's shriveled hand
(Reaction: "Then the Pharisees went out and began to plot with the Herodians how they might kill Jesus.")

In the gospel of Mark the most frequent response to Jesus is surprise, awe, disbelief and fear. "Who is this?" the disciples ask after Jesus calms the waves. This particular question, though phrased differently by different people, is on everybody's lips. The crowds, the scribes, the Pharisees, the high priests, Jesus' friends, Jesus' relatives, the disciples —they all ask it.

Jesus eats with "sinners" and tax collectors. He forgives sins, which is God's exclusive privilege. He cleanses the temple as though he owns the place. He ignores ritual washing. He goes out of his way to break Sabbath rules. He raises people from the dead. In short, he lives by values that run completely counter to the values by which we live. And he asks us to do the same. He asks us to live our lives by God's rules, thereby challenging the status quo.

In Luke 11:27, a woman in the crowd says to Jesus, "Blessed is the mother who gave you birth and nursed you." This sounds like a compliment to Jesus' mother. If we had been part of that crowd, we might have been deeply moved by these words. We might have said, "What a nice thing to say!"

But what sounds like a compliment to Jesus' mother is in reality an indirect way of paying Jesus a compliment. And Jesus, surprisingly, does not take too kindly to it. He does not say, "Thank you, ma'am. I needed that!" Instead, he says, "Blessed rather are those who hear the word of God and obey it."

Here Jesus the parable is speaking, for his reply places the woman in the same position where his parables always place people. Jesus' reply places the well-meaning woman in a situation where she must decide either to leave her old world and its values behind and to move under the kingly rule of God, or to remain in bondage to her old world with its many loyalties. Either she can stay outside the kingdom by admiring Jesus from a distance, or she can enter the kingdom by hearing and obeying Jesus' words.

This is what Jesus' parables do. This is what Jesus the definitive parable does. He shocks and alerts us to the fact that we are placed at the crossroad of two possible choices: continue on as before or follow him into the kingdom.

BIBLIOGRAPHY

The author acknowledges varying degrees of indebtedness to the following works, most of which were quoted or described in the text of this book:

Bailey, Kenneth E. *Poet and Peasant.* Grand Rapids, MI: Eerdmans, 1976.
———. *Through Peasant Eyes.* Grand Rapids, MI: Eerdmans, 1980.
Barclay, William. *And Jesus Said.* Philadelphia: Westminster, 1970.
Brecht, Bertolt. *Short Stories 1921-1946.* New York: Methuen, 1983.
Bornkamm, Günther. *Jesus of Nazareth.* New York: Harper & Row, 1960.
Caird, G. B. *The Language and Imagery of the Bible.* Philadelphia: Westminster, 1980.
Crossan, John Dominic. *In Parables.* San Francisco: Harper & Row, 1973.
———. *The Dark Interval.* Allen, TX: Argus, 1975.
———. *Finding Is the First Act.* Philadelphia: Fortress, 1979.
Croxall, T. H., ed. *Meditations from Kierkegaard.* Philadelphia: Westminster, 1955.
Dodd, C. H. *The Parables of the Kingdom.* London: Collins, 1961.
Drury, John. *The Parables in the Gospels.* New York: Crossroad, 1985.
Funk, Robert W. "How Do You Read?" *Interpretation* 18, (1964): 56-61.
———. "The Old Testament in Parable." *Encounter* 26, no. 2 (1965): 251-267.
———. "The Good Samaritan as Metaphor." *Semeia* 2 (1974): 74-81
Glatzer, Nahum N. *Franz Kafka: The Complete Stories.* New York: Schocken, 1971.
Hawkins, Peter S. "Parable as Metaphor." *Christian Scholar's Review* 12, no. 3 (1983): 226-236.
Hendrickx, Herman. *The Parables of Jesus.* San Francisco: Harper & Row, 1986.
Hunter, Archibald M. *The Parables Then and Now.* Philadelphia: Westminster, 1971.
Jeremias, Joachim. *The Parables of Jesus.* 2nd rev. ed. New York: Scribner, 1954.
Keck, Leander E. *A Future for the Historic Jesus.* Nashville: Abingdon Press, 1971.
Koestler, Arthur. *Janus.* New York: Random House, 1978.
Lambrecht, Jan. *Once More Astonished.* New York: Crossroad, 1976.
Lewis, C. S. *Mere Christianity.* New York: MacMillan, 1943.
Lindsey, Hal. *The Late Great Planet Earth.* Grand Rapids: Zondervan, 1970.
———. *The 1980s: Countdown to Armageddon.* New York: Bantam, 1980.
McFague, Sallie. *Metaphorical Theology.* Philadelphia: Fortress, 1982.

O'Connor, Flannery. *Everything that Rises Must Converge*. New York: Farrar, Straus and Giroux, 1956.

Oesterley, William O. *The Gospel Parables in the Light of Their Jewish Background*. London: Society for Promoting Christian Knowledge, 1938.

Perkins, Pheme. *Hearing the Parables of Jesus*. Ramsey, NJ: Paulist Press, 1981.

Perrin, Norman. *Jesus and the Language of the Kingdom*. Philadelphia: Fortress, 1976.

Ridderbos, Herman. *The Coming of the Kingdom*. St. Catharines, ON: Paideia Press, 1962.

Schillebeeckx, Edward. *God Among Us*. New York: Crossroad, 1983.

Sittler, Joseph. *Gravity and Grace*. Minneapolis: Augsburg, 1986.

Stringfellow, William. *A Simpliciaty of Faith*. Nashville: Abingdon, 1982.

Thielicke, Helmut. *The Waiting Father*. San Francisco: Harper & Row, 1959.

———. *Man in God's World*. New York: Harper & Row, 1963.

von Rad, Gerhard. *Moses*. London: Lutterworth Press, 1960.

Wardlaw, Don M., ed. *Preaching Biblically*. Philadelphia: Westminster, 1983.

Willimon, William H. *Sunday Dinner*. Nashville: The Upper Room, 1981.